DESIGNS ON PREHISTORIC HOPI POTTERY

BY

JESSE WALTER FEWKES

REPRINTED FROM THE THIRTY-THIRD ANNUAL REPORT
OF THE BUREAU OF AMERICAN ETHNOLOGY

WASHINGTON
GOVERNMENT PRINTING OFFICE
1919

23326

CONTENTS

		Page
Introduction		215
Chronology of Hopi pottery symbols		215
The ruin, Sikyatki		218
Sikyatki epoch		219
Human figures		220
Quadruped figures		223
Reptilian figures		225
Winged figures		227
Dorsal views of birds		228
Lateral views of birds		233
Feather designs		236
Feathers suspended from strings		241
Sky-band		242
Vertical attachment to sky-band		243
Birds attached longitudinally to sky-band		246
Decorations on exteriors of food bowls		248
Curved figure with attached feathers		251
Spider and insects		252
Butterfly and moth		252
Geometrical designs		255
Rain clouds		256
Stars		257
Sun emblems		258
Rectangular figures representing shrines		262
Symbols introduced from San Juan River settlements		264
Symbols introduced by the Snake people		265
Tanoan epoch		266
Symbols introduced from the Little Colorado		267
Symbols introduced by the Badger and Kachina clans		273
Symbols introduced from Awatobi		275
Shalako mana		275
Symbols of Hano clans		279
Conclusion		281
Authorities cited		284

ILLUSTRATIONS

PLATES

		Page
76.	Various forms of conventionalized feathers	238
77.	Conventionalized tail feathers	240
78.	Conventionalized feathers attached to strings (nakwakwoci)	240
79.	Sky-bands	242
80.	Geometrical figures on outside of bowls	250
81.	Geometrical figures on outside of bowls	250
82.	Geometrical figures on outside of bowls	250
83.	Geometrical figures on outside of bowls	250
84.	Geometrical figures on outside of bowls	250
85.	Conventionalized bird designs	250
86.	Conventionalized bird designs	250
87.	Bird, sun, and spider and sun symbols	258
88.	Conventionalized bird figures	258
89.	Shalako mana, Corn Maid (from tablet dance)	276
90.	Top of butterfly vase	276

TEXT FIGURES

12.	Human head with hair in characteristic whorls	221
13.	Woman with serpent-like animal	221
14.	Kneeling woman, showing hair in characteristic whorls	222
15.	Three human figures	223
16.	a, Deer; b, rabbit	224
17.	Quadruped	224
18.	Antelope or mountain sheep	224
19.	Mountain lion	225
20.	Problematical reptile	225
21.	Reptile	225
22.	Reptile	225
23.	Reptile	226
24.	Reptile	227
25.	Turtle	227
26.	Clouds and tadpoles	228
27.	Tadpoles	228
28.	Dorsal view of a bird	229
29.	Bird figure, two halves restored to natural position	229
30.	Dorsal view of bird	230
31.	Bird figure	230
32.	Bird figure	231
33.	Bird figure	231
34.	Bird figure	231
35.	Bird figure (Thunderbird)	231
36.	Bird figure	232
37.	Highly conventionalized figure of bird from dorsal side	232
38.	Conventional figure of a bird	233

Page

39. Conventional figure of a bird... 233
40. Conventional figure of a bird... 233
41. Conventional figure of a bird... 233
42. Conventional figure of a bird... 234
43. Triangular form of bird... 234
44. Triangular form of bird... 234
45. Simple form of bird with terraced body.................................. 234
46. Lateral view of triangular bird with two tail feathers................... 234
47. Lateral view of bird with three tail feathers............................ 234
48. Problematical bird figure... 234
49. Bird with two tail feathers.. 234
50. Highly conventionalized bird figure..................................... 234
51. Lateral view of bird... 235
52. Profile of bird.. 235
53. Lateral view of bird with outspread wing................................ 235
54. Lateral view of bird with twisted tail and wing feathers................. 235
55. Lateral view of conventionalized bird................................... 236
56. Lateral view of conventionalized bird................................... 236
57. Feather symbol with black notch... 237
58. Feather symbol with black notch... 237
59. Feathers.. 241
60. Curved feathers... 241
61. Conventional feathers... 241
62. Parallel lines representing feathers.................................... 241
63. Conventionalized bird form hanging from sky-band, top view............. 244
64. Conventionalized bird form hanging from sky-band, top view............. 244
65. Conventionalized bird form hanging from sky-band, top view............. 244
66. Conventionalized bird form hanging from sky-band, top view............. 244
67. Conventionalized bird form hanging from sky-band, top view............. 245
68. Conventionalized bird form hanging from sky-band, top view............. 245
69. Conventionalized bird form hanging from sky-band, top view............. 245
70. Conventionalized bird form hanging from sky-band, top view............. 246
71. Conventionalized bird form hanging from sky-band, top view............. 246
72. Conventionalized bird form hanging from sky-band, top view............. 247
73. Conventionalized bird form hanging from sky-band, top view............. 247
74. Lateral view of bird hanging from sky-band.............................. 247
75. Lateral view of bird hanging from sky-band.............................. 248
76. Lateral view of bird with extended wing................................. 248
77. Lateral view of bird hanging from sky-band.............................. 249
78. Lateral view of bird hanging from sky-band.............................. 249
79. Butterfly and flower.. 252
80. Butterfly with extended proboscis....................................... 253
81. Highly conventionalized butterfly....................................... 253
82. Moth.. 254
83. Moth.. 254
84. Moth of geometrical form.. 255
85. Geometrical form of moth.. 255
86. Highly conventionalized butterfly....................................... 255
87. Geometrical form of moth.. 255
88. Circle with triangles... 255
89. Rain cloud.. 257
90. Rain cloud.. 257
91. Ring with appended feathers... 258

		Page
92.	Two circles with figure	259
93.	Sun with feathers	259
94.	Sun symbol	259
95.	Ring with appended feathers	260
96.	Ring figure with legs and appended feathers	260
97.	Sun emblem with appended feathers	260
98.	Sun symbol	261
99.	Sun symbol	261
100.	Horned snake with conventionalized shrine	263
101.	Shrine	263
102.	Shrine	264
103.	Conventionalized winged bird with shrine	264
104.	Lateral view of bird with double eyes	269
105.	Lateral view of bird with double eyes	270
106.	Bird with double eyes	271
107.	Two birds with rain clouds	272
108.	Head of Shalako mana, or Corn maid	276
109.	Head of Kokle, or Earth woman	280
110.	Head of Hahaiwugti, or Earth woman	280
111.	Ladle with clown carved on handle and Earth woman on bowl	281
112.	Püükon hoya, little War god	281

DESIGNS ON PREHISTORIC HOPI POTTERY

By Jesse Walter Fewkes

INTRODUCTION

In the following pages the author has endeavored to draw attention to some of the most important symbols on Hopi pottery, especially those of prehistoric times.

Consideration of this subject has led to a discussion of the character of pottery designs at different epochs and the interpretation, by study of survivals, of ancient designs in modern times. This chronological treatment has necessitated an examination of ceramic material from ruins of different ages and an ethnological study of ancient symbols still surviving in ceremonials now practiced. It has also led to sociological researches on the composition of the tribe, the sequence in the arrival of clans at Walpi, and their culture in distant homes from which they migrated. It will thus appear that the subject is a very complicated one, and that the data upon which conclusions are based are sociological as well as archeological. There are many ruins from which material might have been obtained, but only a few have been adequately investigated. The small number of ruins in the Hopi country which have thus far been excavated necessarily makes our knowledge not only provisional but also imperfect. It is hoped, however, that this article may serve to stimulate others to renewed field work and so add desired data to the little we have bearing on the subject.

Chronology of Hopi Pottery Symbols

At least three well-marked epochs can be distinguished in the history of Hopi ceramic symbolism. Each of these is intimately associated with certain clans that have from time to time joined the Hopi and whose descendants compose the present population. Although these epochs follow each other in direct sequence, each was not evolved from its predecessor or modified by it, except to a very limited extent. Each epoch has left to the succeeding one a heritage of symbols, survivals which are somewhat difficult to differentiate from exotic symbols introduced by incoming clans. So that while each epoch grades almost imperceptibly into the one directly following it, an abrupt change is sometimes evident in the passage.

In order to appreciate the relations between ceramic decoration and history let me sketch in brief outline what I regard as the historical development of the Hopi living near or on the East Mesa. We know little of the group of people who first settled here except that they belonged to the Bear clan, which is traditionally referred to the eastern pueblo region. At about the time they entered Hopiland there was a settlement called Sikyatki composed of Jemez colonists, situated about 3 miles from the southern point of East Mesa, and other towns or pueblos on Awatobi Mesa and in Antelope Valley, 10 miles away.

The first great additions to this original population were Snake clans, who came from the San Juan, followed by Flute clans from the same direction but originally of southern origin. Having become well established at the point of the East Mesa, the combined settlement overthrew Sikyatki and appropriated its clans.

Then came the strenuous days of Spanish invasion and the destruction of Awatobi in 1700. The Little Colorado clans had already begun to seek refuge in the Hopi mountains and their number was greatly augmented by those from Zuñi, a Rio Grande settlement called Tewadi, and elsewhere, each addition bringing new forms of culture and settling new pueblos on or near the East Mesa, as has been shown in previous publications. Traditions point out their former settlements and it remains for the archeologist to excavate those settlements, now in ruins, and verify these traditions. This can be done by a study of artifacts found in them.

As a rule archeologists have relied on technique, form, and especially color, in the classification of Pueblo pottery, leading, on the technical side, to the groups known as (a) rough, coiled ware, and (b) smooth, polished ware; and on that of form, to bowls, vases, jars, dippers, etc. When color is used as the basis of classification the divisions black and white, red, yellow, orange, and polychrome are readily differentiated. Classifications based on these data are useful, as they indicate cultural as well as geographical differences in Pueblo ceramics; but these divisions can be used only with limitations in a study of stages of culture growth. The fact that they are not emphasized in the present article is not because their importance is overlooked, but rather for the purpose of supplementing them with a classification that is independent of and in some particulars more reliable for indicating chronology and culture distinctions.

The life-forms on ancient Sikyatki and other Hopi pottery are painted on what is known as yellow ware, which is regarded by some authors as characteristic of the Hopi area; but pottery of the same color, yet with radically different symbolic life-forms, occurs also in other areas. It thus appears that while a classification of Pueblo pottery by color is convenient, differences of color are not so much indications of diversity in culture as of geologic environment. Designs on pottery are more comprehensive and more definite in culture studies than color, and are so regarded in these pages.

As there exists a general similarity in the form of prehistoric pottery throughout the Southwest, shape alone is also inadequate for a determination of Pueblo culture centers. The great multiplicity and localization of symbols on Pueblo pottery furnishes adequate material for classification by means of the designs depicted on vases, bowls, and other pottery objects. Sikyatki pottery is especially suited to a classification on such a basis, for it is recognized as the most beautiful and the most elaborately decorated prehistoric pottery found in the Southwest. Life-forms are abundant and their symbolism is sufficiently characteristic to be regarded as typical of a well-defined ceramic area. There can, of course, be no question regarding the ancient character of the designs on Sikyatki pottery, nor were they introduced or modified by white men, but are purely aboriginal and prehistoric.

Pottery from the Sikyatki ruin is chosen as a type of the most highly developed or golden epoch in Hopi ceramics. Several other ruins were inhabited when Sikyatki was in its prime and pottery from these belongs to the same epoch, and would probably be equally good to illustrate its character. Fortunately, specimens are available from many of these, as Awatobi, and the ruins in Antelope Valley, old Shumopavi, and other Middle Mesa ruins. The date of the origin of this epoch, or the highest development of Hopi ceramics, is not known, but there is evidence that it lasted until the fall of Awatobi, in 1700. The destruction of Sikyatki occurred before 1540, but Sikyatki has given the name to the epoch and is taken as the type, not only because of the abundance of ceramic material available from that ruin, but also because there can be no doubt of the prehistoric nature of material from it.

There is abundant evidence that the culture of Sikyatki was never influenced by white man. After the overthrow of Awatobi there developed on the East Mesa of the Hopi country a third ceramic epoch which was largely influenced by the influx of Tanoan (Tewa) clans. They came either directly from the Rio Grande or by way of Zuñi and other pueblos. Among other arrivals about 1710 were those clans which settled Hano, a Tewa pueblo on the East Mesa. The Hano and other symbols introduced in this epoch are best known in the present generation by the earlier productions of Nampeo, an expert modern potter.

The pottery of this epoch differs from that of the second in form, color, and technique, but mainly in its symbolism, which is radically different from that of the epochs that preceded it. The symbolism of this phase is easily determined from large collections now in museums. This epoch was succeeded in 1895 by a fourth, in which there was a renaissance of old Sikyatki patterns, under the lead of Nampeo. In that year Nampeo visited the excavations at Sikyatki and made pencil copies of the designs on mortuary bowls. From that time all pottery manufactured by her was decorated with modified Sikyatki symbols, largely to meet the demand for this beautiful ancient ware. The extent of her work, for which there was a large demand, may be judged by the great numbers of Hopi bowls displayed in every Harvey store from New Mexico to California. This modified Sikyatki ware, often sold by unscrupulous traders as ancient, is the fourth, or present, epoch of Hopi ceramics. These clever imitations, however, are not as fine as the productions of the second epoch. There is danger that in a few years some of Nampeo's imitations will be regarded as ancient Hopi ware of the second epoch, and more or less confusion introduced by the difficulty in distinguishing her work from that obtained in the ruins.

THE RUIN, SIKYATKI

The ruins of the ancient pueblo of Sikyatki, consisting of mounds and a few outcropping walls, are situated on rocky elevations rising from the sand hills at the eastern or sunny base of the East Mesa, about 3 miles from the modern Hopi pueblo of Walpi in northeastern Arizona. The founders of Sikyatki are said, in very circumstantial migration legends, to have belonged to a [Keres?] clan called the Kokop, or Firewood, which previously lived in a pueblo near Jemez, New Mexico. Preliminary excavations were made at Sikyatki, under the author's direction, by the Smithsonian Institution in 1895, when there was obtained, chiefly from its cemeteries, a valuable collection of pottery, most of which is now installed in the National Museum.[1]

Little is known of the history of Sikyatki save through tradition, but enough has been discovered to show that it was abandoned before 1540, the year of the visit to Tusayan of Pedro Tovar, an officer of the Coronado expedition. It was probably settled much earlier, perhaps about the time the Bear clans, also said to have come from the Jemez region, built the first houses of Walpi near the point of the terrace at the west or cold side of the East Mesa, below the present settlement.[2] Both of these prehistoric pueblos occupied sites exposed

---

[1] A report on the field work at Sikyatki will be found in the *Seventeenth Ann. Rept. Bur. Amer. Ethn.*, part 2.

[2] Traces of the ancient village of Walpi at this point are still to be seen, and certain ancestral ceremonies are still performed here, in the New-fire rites, as elsewhere described.

to attack by enemies and were not built on mesa tops, hence it may be assumed that there were no enemies to fear in Tusayan at the time of their establishment. But later, when the Snake clans from the north joined the Bear settlement at Walpi, trouble seems to have commenced. As above mentioned, the Bear clans came from the same region as the Kokop and were presumably friendly, probably kin of the Sikyatkians; but the Snake clans came from Tokonabi, in the north, and were no doubt of foreign stock, implying a hostility that may have been the indirect cause of the overthrow of Sikyatki and Awatobi by the other Hopi.

The two epochs in Hopi ceramic development that can be distinguished with certainty are (1) the Sikyatki epoch and (2) the Tanoan or historic epoch. The third, or renaissance, of the Sikyatki dates back to 1895, and may be called the modern epoch. The Sikyatki epoch gave way to the Tanoan about the beginning of the eighteenth century. It did not develop from any group preexisting in the neighborhood of the present Hopi pueblos but was derived from the east and it ceased suddenly, being replaced by a totally different group introduced by radically different clans.[1]

SIKYATKI EPOCH

The most characteristic Hopi pottery bearing symbols of the Sikyatki epoch occurs in a few ruins near the Hopi mesas, but from lack of exploration it is impossible to determine the boundaries of the area in which it is found.

Several museums contain collections of Hopi ware of this epoch, among which may be mentioned the National Museum at Washington, the Field Columbian Museum of Natural History at Chicago, the Museum of the University of Pennsylvania, the Peabody Museum at Cambridge, and the Museum für Volkerkünde at Berlin, Germany. Many bowls of this epoch are likewise found in the American Museum of Natural History, New York, and in the Museum of the Brooklyn Institute. Several private collections in Europe and the United States likewise contain specimens of Sikyatki ware, among them being that gathered by the late Dr. Miller, now at Phoenix, Arizona. The collection of prehistoric Hopi pottery in the National Museum is particularly rich, containing many specimens gathered by the Stevenson expeditions, by the author, and by Dr. Hough, of the U. S. National Museum.

The symbols on the ancient pottery from the Middle Mesa of the Hopi are almost identical with those of Sikyatki, indicating a similarity of culture, a common geographical origin, and a synchronous

---

[1] Pottery making is a woman's industry, and as among the Pueblo the woman determines the clan, so she determines the symbolism of the pottery. Consequently symbolism of pottery is related to that of the clan.

culture. From the character of the symbols on the ancient pottery from the ancient Middle Mesa pueblos it is probable that the clans who founded them came, like the colonists who settled Sikyatki, from the Jemez plateau in New Mexico. Although the Field collection is very rich in old Walpi ware, nothing of importance has been published on the symbols of this collection; it contains some of the most instructive examples of the Sikyatki epoch. A large and probably the most valuable portion of this collection was gathered by Dr. George A. Dorsey and Mr. Charles L. Owen, while many pieces were purchased from Mr. Frank Wattron, of Holbrook, and from the late Mr. T. V. Keam, of Keams Canyon, Arizona. The source of many of the Wattron specimens is unknown, but it is evident from their decoration that some of them are ancient Hopi and probably belong to the Sikyatki epoch and came from Shongopovi, Awatobi, or Sikyatki.

Shortly before his death Mr. T. V. Keam sold to the Museum für Volkerkünde at Berlin, Germany, a rich collection of pottery obtained mainly from Awatobi and Sikyatki, containing several specimens of the Sikyatki epoch which are highly instructive. Some of the designs on the pottery of this collection are unique, and their publication would be a great aid to a study of the most important epoch of Hopi ceramics.

A large proportion of life-forms used in the decoration of Sikyatki pottery are mythological subjects, showing the predominance of supernatural beings and their magic power in the minds of the makers. Like a child, the primitive artist is fond of complexity of detail, and figures in which motion is indicated appealed more to his fancy than those objects that do not move. It needs but a glance at the ancient Sikyatki life-figures to show a tendency to represent detail and to convince one of the superiority of the Sikyatki potters in this respect over those of modern times. There has been a gradual deterioration, not only less care being now devoted to the technique of the pottery but also to the drawing of the figures. This lack in itself is significant, for while modern ware reflects in its hasty crudeness the domination of commercialism, the ancient pottery shows no indication of such influence. Pottery is now made to please the purchaser; in ancient times another motive influenced the maker, for then it was a product worthy of the highest use to which it could be put, since it often formed a part of sacred paraphernalia in religious ceremonies.

HUMAN FIGURES

Sikyatki pictures of human beings depict men and women, singly or in company, and are few in number and crude in execution. Or-

gans of the body—hands, feet, arms, and legs—are often represented separately. The hand is portrayed on two vessels, and the foot,
elaborately drawn, appears on another; as a general thing when parts of the body are represented they are greatly conventionalized. The few human figures on Sikyatki pottery are crude representations as compared with those of animals, and especially of birds. Several of the figures are represented wearing ancient costumes and ornaments, and one or two have their hair done up in unusual styles; others have the body or face tattooed or painted; but as a whole these decorations are rare and shed little light

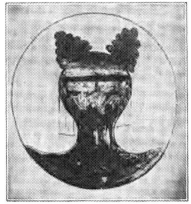

FIG. 12. — Human head with hair in characteristic whorls.

on prehistoric customs. There is nothing that can be identified as a time count, calendric, hieroglyphic, or phonetic signs, or any record of historical events.

None of the human figures are represented with masks or head-

FIG. 13.—Woman with serpent-like animal.

dresses to indicate the impersonation of kachinas, nor are there double figures or animal heads depicted on human bodies. The absence of animal or kachina heads shows one of the marked differences between Sikyatki pictures and the designs so common on some other pottery, where a relatively large number of the heads of the latter occur. The best representation of a human head is shown in figure 12,[1] in which a characteristic coiffure is shown. Fig 13 is identified as a figure of a maiden whose hair is dressed in two whorls, one above each ear, like a modern Hopi maid.[2] Opposite this maid is a reptile or similar animal with

---

[1] Many of the illustrations appearing in this paper are taken from the author's memoir on the results of the Sikyatki excavations in the *17th Ann. Rep. Bur. Amer. Ethnol.*, part 2.

[2] Hopi maidens dress their hair in two whorls, one above each ear, which on marriage are taken down and braided in two coils. There are differences in the style of putting up the hair, as appear in different ceremonial personages, but the custom of wearing it in whorls was probably general among ancient Pueblo maidens and is still followed in certain ceremonial dances in which women are personated by men. For the difference in the style of the whorls, see the author's series of pictures of Hopi kachinas in the *Twenty-first Ann. Rept. Bur. Amer. Eth.*

head decorated with two eyes on one side and a single foreleg. These two figures probably refer to some episode or Indian legend connecting a Sikyatki maiden with some monster.

The maiden depicted in figure 14 is evidently kneeling, her knees being brought together below, and separated by four median parallel lines that are supposed to indicate feathers; the curved objects at the lower corners of the rectangular blanket probably are also feathers. One hand of the maiden is raised to her head, while the other holds an unknown object, possibly an ear of corn. The woman with an ear of corn recalls a figure on the elaborately painted wooden slab carried by women in the Hopi Marau dance or that on the wooden slab, or *monkohu*, carried by the priests representing Alosaka, Eototo, and other ceremonial personages. These painted slabs do not always

Fig. 14.—Kneeling woman, showing hair in characteristic whorls.

bear pictures of corn ears, for those of the priests known as the Aaltu have, instead of pictures of corn, the corn itself tied to them; in the New-fire ceremony at Walpi members of the Tataukyamû priesthood, at Walpi, also hold ears of corn with or without wooden slabs, while those borne by the warrior Kwakwantû are carved in the form of the sacred plumed serpent, which is their patron.[1]

Different styles of hairdressing are exhibited in figures 13 and 14, that of figure 14 being similar to the modern Hopi. The group of three figures (fig. 15) possibly illustrates some ancient ceremony. The middle figure of this group is represented as carrying a branched stick, or cornstalk, in his mouth.[2] The accompanying figure, or that to the right, has in his hand one of the strange frames used as rattles[3] in historic times by clans (Asa or Honani) of Jemez or of Tewa descent who had settled at the East Mesa. The author is inclined to identify the object held by this figure as one of these ceremonial frames and the man as a Yaya priest.

---

[1] The best idol of this god known to the author appears on one of the Flute altars at Oraibi. It has a single horn (representing the serpent horn) on the head, two wings, and two legs with lightning symbols their whole length. The horned plumed Lightning god of the Kwakwantû at Walpi is represented by plumed serpent effigies in the March ceremony or dramatisation elsewhere described.

[2] In the Antelope dance at Walpi, a stalk of corn instead of a snake is carried in the mouth on the day before the Snake dance. (Fewkes, Snake Ceremonials at Walpi, pp. 73–74.)

[3] For descriptions of similar objects see Fewkes, Hopi Ceremonial Frames from Cañon de Chelly, Arizona, pp. 664–670; Fewkes, The Lesser New-fire Ceremony at Walpi, p. 438, pl. XI; also *Twenty-first Ann. Rept. Bur. Amer. Eth.*, pls. XXXIV, XXXV.

Another interpretation of the central figure of the group, figure 15, is that he is performing the celebrated stick-swallowing act which was practiced at Walpi until a few years ago. The last explanation suggested implies that the human figures represent Snake and Antelope priests, a doubtful interpretation, since, according to legends, these priests were never represented at Sikyatki.[1]

The character shown in another figure, not copied, may represent the supernatural being, called the God of the Dead (Masauû) whose body, according to legend, is spotted and girt by bands. The Little Fire god (Shulewitse), when personated in modern ceremonies of the Tewa at Hano, is represented by a man daubed with pigments of several colors. He is personated likewise in the Hopi (Tewa) village of Sichomovi.[2]

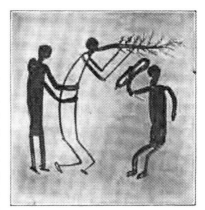

FIG. 15.—Three human figures.

Several Zuñi ceremonies show evidence of derivation from eastern New Mexican pueblos,[3] but a critical examination of the origin and migration of Zuñi clan relations of societies still awaits the student of this interesting pueblo. It is probable that Zuñi sociology is in some respects like that of Walpi and that the present population is composite, having descended from clans which have drifted together from different directions, each bringing characteristic ceremonies and mythological conceptions, while certain rites have been incorporated from time to time from other Pueblo people.

QUADRUPED FIGURES

Representations of quadrupeds are almost as rare as human figures in Sikyatki pottery decorations. The deer (fig. 16, a), antelope, mountain sheep, mountain lion, rabbit, and one or two other animals are recognizable, but pictures of these are neither so common nor so highly conventionalized as those of birds.

[1] As a matter of history, the Snake people of Walpi may have been hostile to the Kokop of Sikyatki on account of linguistic or tribal differences which culminated in the destruction of the latter pueblo in prehistoric times.

[2] The pueblo of Sichomovi, called by the Hopi Sioki, or Zuñi pueblo, was settled by Asa clans, who were apparently of exotic origin but who went to Sichomovi from Zuñi, in which pueblo the Asa people are known as Aiyahokwe. The Sichomovi people still preserve Zuñi ceremonies and Zuñi kachinas, although they now speak the Hopi language— an example of a pueblo in which alien ceremonies and personations have survived or been incorporated, although its language has been superseded by another.

[3] Thus the Heyamashikwe may be supposed to have originally come from Jemez. The Zuñi Sumaikoli, like that of the Hopi, is practically Tewa in origin.

Figure 17 shows one of two mammalian figures on a bowl, the surrounding surface consisting of spatterwork, an uncommon but effective mode of treatment.

The outline of the animal shown in figure 18 is intensified by spattering, as in the case of the animal last mentioned. The black spots

along the back and tail are absent in other figures. The design below the figure suggests, in some particulars, that of a highly conventionalized shrine, but its true meaning is unknown.

FIG. 16.—a, Deer; b, rabbit.

The design in figure 19 has been regarded as representing a mountain lion, but there is some doubt of the validity of this identification. Although the feet are like those of a carnivorous animal, the head is not. The two projections from the head, which may represent horns, are not unlike those associated with the two figures next described, which have been regarded as feathers.

FIG 17.—Quadruped.

FIG. 18.—Antelope or mountain sheep.

The creature shown in figure 20 is also problematical. The appendages to the head are prolonged, terminating in feathers that bend backward and touch the body. The anterior body appendage has two crescentic prolongations between which are parallel lines of unequal length. The posterior limb is jointed, the lower half extending backward and terminating in two claws, one long, the other short. Between these extensions are two groups of slightly radiating lines that may be regarded as feathers. The body has feathers like those of a highly conventionalized bird, while the limbs resemble those of a lizard. The body is serpentine, and tail feathers are wanting; both legs have talons like those of birds, and the appendage to the head suggests a feather headdress; the line connecting the head appendage and one claw of the posterior limbs recalls a sky-band, commonly found in representations of sky gods.

The animal depicted in figure 21, which resembles figure 19 in the

Fɪɢ. 19.—Mountain lion.

Fɪɢ. 20.—Problematical reptile.

form of the appendages to the head and mouth, is suspended inside of a circle in the one case and is half within a circle in the other.

Reptilian Figures

Several figures of reptiles and serpents occur in the Sikyatki collection. Figure 22 represents an animal like a reptile; only two legs

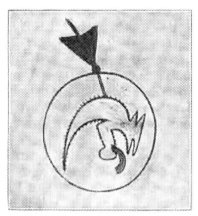

Fɪɢ. 21.—Reptile.

Fɪɢ. 22.—Reptile.

are shown in the design and the form of the tail recalls that of a bird. The head of this figure bears two horns resembling feathers in some respects; the legs terminate in four claws. From a projection at the posterior end of the body there arises a curved line dotted at intervals and terminating in feathers. The dorsal appendage resembles the carapace of a turtle, from beneath which feathers project.

Figure 22 depicts a reptile from the head of which project horns and two long feathers. Its back bears a row of feathers, but it has only two legs.

The legless creature, figure 23, has two triangular earlike feathers rising from the head, and two eyes; a wide-open mouth, in which are six long, curved teeth, three in each jaw. The tongue terminates in an arrow-shaped figure, recalling a conventional symbol of lightning, or the death-dealing power of the serpent. The meaning of the narrow line connecting the upper jaw with the tail is not known. The curved shape of the body of the reptile is necessitated by the shape of the bowl on which it is drawn. This figure may represent the monster feathered serpent of Sikyatki, or a flying reptile, one of the most mysterious of the elemental gods. It is interesting to note that while the effigies of the feathered serpent used in Hopi (Walpi) and Zuñi religious practices has a single horn on the head, the one here described is different from both, for it is provided with two appendages resembling conventionalized feathers. The Hopi feathered serpent was derived from the same source as the Zuñi, namely, clans which originally came to the Little Colorado from Gila Valley.[1]

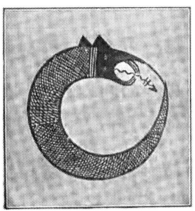

FIG. 23.—Reptile.

The Hopi (Walpi) figure is in a measure comparable with that shown in figure 23—each has two hornlike feathers on the head, and the bodies are curved in the same direction—that is, with the center (?) on the right (dextral circuit), the reverse of modern Hopi pictures, which are placed as if the figures were moving in a sinistral circuit.[2]

The form shown in figure 24 reminds one of a frog or a turtle. The body and feet are turtlelike. As in several pictures of reptiles, it is provided with an anterior appendage, evidently the front leg, which has characteristic claws. The row of white dots extending from the mouth through the neck represents the esophagus or windpipe. The author is unable to offer any interpretation of the append-

---

[1] See Fewkes, The Butterfly in Hopi Myth and Ritual, pp. 576–594.
[2] The clay images representing the Tewa plumed serpent on the Winter Solstice altar at Hano have rows of feathers inserted along their backs (as in the case of the reptile shown in figure 22) as well as rudimentary horns, teeth made of corn kernels, and necklaces of the same. (Fewkes, Winter solstice altars at Hano pueblo, pp. 269–270.) A mosaic of corn kernels on a clay base (kaetukwi) is known in ceremonies derived from Sikyatki and Awatobi.

ages to the tail, but suggests that they may have been intended for feathers. Figure 25 *a*, *b*, is identified as a turtle.

Figure 26 was evidently designed to represent several tadpoles swimming across a bowl between rows of rain clouds, the whole inclosed in a circle to which are attached five stars at approximately equal intervals. The form of the rain clouds reminds one of conventional tail feathers. There are six of these rain-cloud figures on one side of the field of decoration and five on the other. The tadpoles shown in figure 27 occur on the inside of the ladle.

FIG. 24.—Reptile.

WINGED FIGURES

The term "winged figures" is here employed to designate all flying creatures, as birds, insects, and bats, even though they belong zoologically to different groups of animals. Among the prehistoric Hopi, insects and birds were designated by similar symbols and when highly conventionalized sometimes merge into one another. It was the custom of Sikyatki potters to give more attention to specific than generic characters of flying creatures, distinguishing different kinds of birds by the form of their feathers. The symbol of a turkey, an eagle, or a hawk feather was distinct from that of an owl, and each kind of a bird had its own special symbolic marking, especially indicated in the different kinds of feathers. Thus it occurs that Sikyatki bird designs, instead of being realistically represented, are often so highly conventionalized that the genus can not be identified.

a   *b*
FIG. 25.—Turtle.

The flight of birds, like the movement of serpents, is regarded as mysterious, and anything mysterious or uncanny has always profoundly affected the mind of primitive man. The chief visible characteristics connected with the flight of a bird are wings and feathers, and the kind of feathers of a particular bird led to their association with the supposed magic power of the bird itself among both the ancient and modern Hopi. Different kinds of feathers have different powers; thus the feathers of the turkey, for example, among the modern Hopi, are potent in inducing rain; those of the eagle or the hawk pertain especially to the power of the sun; a breast feather of

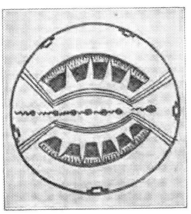

FIG. 26.—Clouds and tadpoles.

an eagle is chosen as an individual prayer bearer. The feathers of an owl, like the owl itself,[1] are generally regarded as having a sinister influence; but sometimes the feather of this bird is beneficial, it is believed, in making peach trees yield abundantly. From the variety of feather designs and the frequency with which they occur in modern Hopi ceremonies [2] it is evident that the Sikyatki people, like their descendants, attributed special magic power to different kinds of these objects.

In their simplest forms bird symbols are little more than triangles, the tail feathers being represented by appended parallel lines, which are mere suggestions of birds and may be designated as cursive forms. Such simple pictures of birds sometimes have, in addition to the appended parallel lines referred to, an angular or a curved line or hook extending from one of the angles of the triangle to represent a beak. Such triangular bird figures may be free or attached; in the latter case they are suspended from other figures or rise from the corners of a rectangular design when one of the triangles may be without tail or beak appendages, another may have parallel lines, while a third may take a form readily recognizable as that of a bird. The form of the beak and the claws of bird figures also varies, the claws often appearing

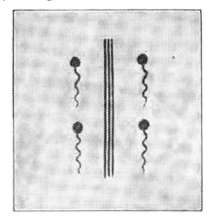

FIG. 27.—Tadpoles.

as simple crosses or crescents. The beak is sometimes toothed, often hooked like that of a raptorial bird. The bird is designated by the combination of the beak, claws, and body, as well as the feathers.

DORSAL VIEWS OF BIRDS

Among the conventional pictures of birds on Sikyatki pottery some are shown as seen from above, or dorsally, others from below, or

---

[1] The hoot of the owl portends disaster among the Hopi, as among the ancient Greeks.
[2] Every priest has a box in which his feathers are preserved until needed.

ventrally, and still others laterally. These pictures sometimes become so conventionalized that it is difficult to identify the parts represented, as will appear from illustrations to follow.

Figure 28 represents a bird design in which three parallel bands representing tail feathers of a well-marked type hang between two curved extensions that occupy the relative position of wings. In the angles near the attachment of these tail feathers there are two globular enlargements which occur also in other pictures. The extremity of each winglike crescent is spirally curved inward. Two semicircular figures representing rain clouds are surmounted by two parallel lines and a heavy, solid band, appearing at the proximal end of the tail in the position where the body should end, as in other figures where the rain-cloud symbols are much more complex.

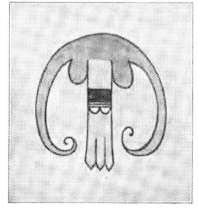

Fɪɢ. 28.—Dorsal view of a bird.

The two drawings shown in figure 29 are the two halves of a single figure cut along its medial line. One of these halves is reversed in such a way that corresponding parts are found on the same side. Viewing these two parts in this position, we can readily identify various organs of a highly conventionalized bird whose wings are represented by a curved body terminating in a spiral, the body decorated with rain-cloud figures and the bowl with conventionalized figures. This is the only figure showing the distortions and reversions of the two halves of the bird's body and appendages.

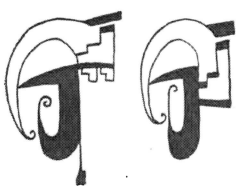

Fɪɢ. 29.—Bird figure, two halves restored to natural position.

Homologous parts are recognizable also in the bird design shown in figure 30, but in this picture the size of the wings is greatly reduced, each consisting merely of two feathers. The rectangular body bears a single large terraced or rectangular rain-cloud symbol, three semicircular figures, and two triangles. Two tail feathers and two posterior extensions of the body, one on each side, are shown. There are three parallel lines on each side of these posterior extensions. In a bird design, figure 31, the body is decorated with four triangular rain clouds and the wings are extended. The tail has six feathers with a lateral extension on each side. The two detached figures asso-

FIG. 30.—Dorsal view of a bird.

ciated with this bird design possibly were intended to represent the shrines of these birds.

The curved appendages are spreading in figure 32, and at their point of junction with the body arises a typical feather symbol. The body has four solid semicircular figures, possibly representing rain clouds, and a single feather on the top of the head. Organs corresponding to wings, body, and tail are traceable, but they are somewhat modified in comparison with the forms already considered. This design is partly surrounded by a band to which two star designs are attached.

We find all the parts or organs associated with the bird designs already described represented in figure 33, but the details of the symbolism are more elaborated than in any of the preceding. Here the wings are bent inward, while the feathers have taken more angular forms. The head is rectangular, bearing representations of two rain clouds just above the wings, while two others appear below. These have the same form as the cloud symbols shown in figure 20. Although this drawing is far from being a realistic representation of a bird, the presence of symbols characteristic of certain avian features leaves no doubt that a bird was intended.

In figure 34 is shown a Sikyatki bird figure still further conventionalized, but the parts are depicted in such manner as to make the

FIG. 31.—Bird figure.

identification as a bird practically certain. Head, body, wings, and tail are elaborately represented. The head is semicircular and surmounted by a headdress with three vertical feathers. The wings are large, each terminating in two symbols representing the feathers,[1] with pointed distal extremities. The tail feathers have rounded ex-

---

[1] Compare with feathers, pl. 90, d.

tremities and are three in number. On each side of the feathers of
the headdress, wings, and tail hang figures of unknown meaning.
This is one of the most instructive bird figures in the collection from
Sikyatki.

Figure 35 represents a very elaborate figure of a bird, readily
comparable with the last mentioned, from which it differs in certain

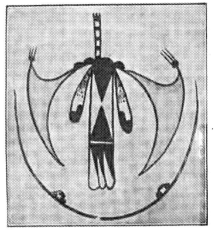

FIG. 32.—Bird figure.

FIG. 33.—Bird figure.

particulars. This bird design is replete with symbolism and may
be regarded as one of the most instructive pictures that has come to
us from the ancient Hopi. The view is from the back, the legs being

FIG. 34.—Bird figure.

FIG. 35.—Bird figure.   (Thunderbird.)

much reduced in size, the claws alone being represented at each upper
corner of the body directly under the attachment of the wings. The
beak is invisible, but an elaborate headdress,[1] in which tail feathers

---

[1] Probably the serrated circle to which the headdress is attached was not designed as the
outline of the head, but the headband turned out of perspective.

are conspicuous, is a prominent feature. The form of the tail and wing feathers of this bird is practically the same as the last, except that they are more elaborately drawn. Each wing has two feathers, and three others form the tail. The arrow points projecting from beneath the extremities of the wing feathers are possibly lightning symbols. Each is crossed by two bars in the same manner as the tongue projecting from the mouth of the serpent shown in figure 23, which is also a lightning symbol.

FIG. 86.—Bird figure.

The design illustrated in figure 36 represents a bird, as seen from the back, with outstretched wings, recalling the lateral view of a bird shown in figure 54 in having smaller bird figures attached to the tips of the wings. The place of attachment of the wings to the body is embellished with crosshatched lines and stepped figures, recalling the rain-cloud symbols. The head is rectangular, destitute of a beak, inclosing two square figures with short parallel lines, representing falling rain, projecting from the upper side. On one side of the head is a semicircular design. The tail has three feathers, the two on the sides being broader than the one in the middle. These feathers are without markings, but the end of the body from which they depend is ornamented with stepped figures surmounted by two horizontal parallel lines and two triangles. In the background, at each side of the body, there are dotted circles, suggesting flowers, a feature often accompanying designs representing butterflies or moths.

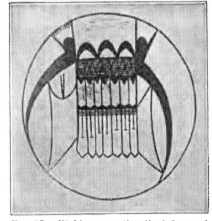

FIG. 37.—Highly conventionalized figure of bird from dorsal side.

In figure 37 is shown a highly conventionalized dorsal view of a bird, with sickle-formed wings slightly extended, seven pointed tail feathers with lateral appendages, and a rectangular head with three semicircular rain-cloud figures. The globular enlargement at the base of the wings in one instance is accompanied by a fan-shaped figure.

The design shown in figure 38 is regarded as a highly conventionalized bird symbol, each wing being represented by a curved pendant,
to the extremities of which feathers
are attached. The body is rectangular and decorated with a median
horizontal white band continued
above and below into black lateral
triangles which possibly may represent feathers, and flanked triangular white areas on each side.

Fɪɢ. 38.—Conventional figure of a bird.

In figure 39 the
design has been
so greatly con-
ventionalized
that almost all
resemblance to a bird has been lost. The wings
are represented by simple terraces, the body by a
rectangular figure, and the head terminates in
three points. It is possible that the limit of bird
conventionalization has been reached in this variant, and the difficulty of identification of organs is
correspondingly great.

Fɪɢ. 39.—Conventional
figure of a bird.

The design shown in figure 40 would perhaps
more logically fall within the series of circular
figures, identified as sun em-
blems, elsewhere considered, ex-
cept for the extensions representing wings and tail.
This is mentioned as one of the instances where
organs of birds are combined with a circle to represent the Sun god.

Figure 41 resembles
figure 40 in some essential
points and may also be
considered in connection
with sun emblems. On
account of the presence of feathers it is
here included among the bird designs.

Fɪɢ. 40.—Conven-
tional figure of a
bird.

Figure 42 exhibits an exceptional bird
form as viewed from the rear.[1] Wings,
body, tail, and possibly the head, are recognized after some study.

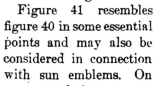

Fɪɢ. 41.—Conventional figure
of a bird.

LATERAL VIEWS OF BIRDS

Drawings representing side views of birds are usually highly conventionalized, often taking the forms of simple geometric figures,

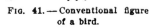

---

[1] See *Seventeenth Ann. Rept. Bur. Amer. Ethn.*, pt. 2, pl. ᴄxʟɪ, *a*. A circle is here drawn
on each side of the bird.

as shown in figures 43–45. The simplest representation of a bird viewed from the side is a triangle, but another, slightly elaborated

FIG. 42.—Conventional figure of a bird.

and a little more complicated (fig. 43), consists of a triangular body with curved lines representing a head and beak, extending from one of the angles, and with two short lines indicating a feathered head crest. The head of the bird shown in figure 44 resembles a section of a Greek fret, which in figure 45 has become still further simplified. Figure 46 represents a bird with triangular body and key-shaped head. Figure 47 shows a similar design, except that the body is partly rectangular, with breast slightly concave. The body in figure 48 is simply an outline of a terrace and the tail is indicated by five parallel lines.

FIG. 43.—Triangular form of bird.

The bird design shown in profile in figure 49 is realistic, all the parts being clearly recognizable. This figure is one of four, each attached to a corner of a rectangle.

FIG. 44.—Triangular form of bird.

FIG. 45.—Simple form of bird with terraced body.

FIG. 46.—Lateral view of triangular bird with two tail feathers.

Another figure which may be a lateral view of a bird is represented in figure 50, in which the part representing the head is curved, the body square, and two obliquely twisted feathers represent the tail.

FIG. 47.—Lateral view of bird with three tail feathers.

FIG. 48.—Problematical bird figure.

FIG. 49.—Bird with two tail feathers.

This figure exhibits avian features more obscurely than those already considered, but the head and the tail feathers are quite birdlike.

In figure 51 is shown a lateral view of a bird, seemingly in flight, the head and beak of which are birdlike. The wings, feet, head, and

FIG. 50.—Highly conventionalized bird figure.

body are not difficult to recognize. Two legs and one wing are shown, and the well-drawn tail, terminating in white-tipped feathers, suggests the turkey, which bird is regarded by the modern Hopi as so efficacious in bringing rain that its feathers are employed in almost all rain ceremonies. The author has seen a similar drawing on altar and other ceremonial paraphernalia among the Hopi priests of the present day. The white tips which characterize the tail feathers of the turkey originated, according to a Hopi legend, at the time when this bird dragged the end of its tail in the mud after a flood had subsided.

FIG. 51.—Lateral view of bird.

The bird shown in figure 52 has a curved, elongated beak, a more or less angular body, two legs, and two small wings. The tail consists of three feathers[1] with characteristic projections.

One of the best bird pictures on Sikyatki pottery is shown in figure 53. The body is somewhat triangular in shape and the wing is spread out, here shown above the back; the tail is provided

FIG. 52.—Profile of bird.

with three feathers placed vertically instead of horizontally, and bent over at their ends into triangles, evidently owing to the lack of available space. The beak is characteristically curved; the single eye is provided with a pupil. The long

FIG. 53.—Lateral view of bird with outspread wing.

FIG. 54.—Lateral view of bird with twisted tail and wing feathers.

claws, single on each foot, suggest an eagle, hawk, or other raptorial bird. The spiral appendage to the under rim of the tail is of unknown meaning.

The design shown in figure 54 is one of the most complex bird drawings found on Sikyatki pottery. The head is triangular, with an eye situated in the center, and the beak continued into a very large, elaborate fret. The body is rhomboidal in shape, the upper portion being occupied by a patterned square. Rising above the

[1] It is, of course, only a coincidence that so many of the Sikyatki bird designs have three tail feathers like Egyptian representations

body is a conventionalized wing, while depending from its lowermost angle is a diminutive figure resembling feathers. The tail consists of two elongate feathers, rounded at their outer ends and fused at the point of union with the body.

Having seen how prone the ancient Hopi were to represent birds on their pottery and the extent to which conventionalization of these fig-

ures prevailed, one finds many designs so closely related to known bird figures that the tendency is to include with them many the identification of which is doubtful. Certain simple geometrical forms originally derived from bird designs were copied by these early potters, presumably without intending to represent birds, but rather merely as decorative motives. Two of these problematic designs are shown in figures 55 and 56.

Fig. 55.—Lateral view of conventionalized bird.

FEATHER DESIGNS

A large number of conventional figures representing feathers have been identified, but there are many others which yet remain to be interpreted, and the particular genus of birds to which each should be referred is likewise problematical. There is no doubt, from a study of the uses of different kinds of feathers in modern Hopi ceremonials, that each form depicted on pottery represents a feather which played an important rôle in ancient Hopi rituals.

Many unquestionable feather designs pictured on Sikyatki pottery are found

Fig. 56.—Lateral view of conventionalized bird.

depicted on serpents, or are attached to inanimate objects, such as rainbows, clouds, and lightning.

It is probable that the majority of feather designs on ancient Hopi earthenware are included in the following types, to which no doubt other forms of feather designs will be added later. These types are abundant in vessels of the Sikyatki epoch.

From the above pictures of birds and many others it may be seen that feather symbols assume a variety of forms in sikyatki pottery decoration. There are probably more than 50 different designs, each representing a different kind of feather, and implying for each a distinct use or ceremonial efficacy, as among the modern Hopi. Our knowledge of ancient Hopi symbolism is not yet sufficient to enable us to identify all the different birds to which these various forms of feathers belong, nor do we know the uses to which all these feathers were put.[1]

FIG. 57. — Feather symbol with black notch.

Several wooden slabs and idols on Hopi altars have features drawn upon them, and many ceremonial sand-pictures contain designs representing feathers. In rare instances, as in the altar of the Powamû,[2] typical Sikyatki symbols of feathers are still used, but feather symbols of a form not found on Sikyatki pottery far outnumber those from that ruin. The existence of one type of Sikyatki feathers on the figure of Pokema in kachina altars may point to the derivation of this feather symbol from Sikyatki, but some of these types are widespread.[3]

The forms assumed by feathers on Sikyatki pottery may best be presented by considering a few examples of the more common types.

FIG. 58. — Feather symbol with black notch.

Figure 57 represents an unusual type of feather symbol, readily distinguished from others by the notch at the end, the edge of which is commonly rounded. There are two subdivisions of this type, one with a dotted shaft (fig. 58), the other plain. This form of feather design is found in most unexpected associations, occurring on the heads of serpents or attached to various parts of the body and under the wings of birds. It also hangs from diametrical bands drawn across the inside of food bowls and from other objects constituting the decoration of vessels. In a few instances this type of feather is enlarged and constitutes the essential part of the design, with other symbols attached.

---

[1] Feathers are among the most important objects employed in Pueblo ceremonies, and among the modern Hopi feathers of different birds are regarded as efficacious for different specific purposes. Thus the turkey feather symbol is efficacious to bring rain, and the hawk and eagle feathers are potent in war. The specific feather used ceremonially by modern Hopi priests is regarded by them as of great importance, and the same doubtless was true of the priests of ancient Sikyatki and Awatobi. Belief in a difference in the magic power of certain feathers was deeply rooted in the primitive mind, and was regarded as of great importance by the ancient as well as the modern Hopi.

[2] Compare the sand-mosaic of the sun associated with the Powalawû altar of Oraibi, and the sun emblem shown in fig. 98.

[3] Mallery (*Fourth Ann. Rept. Bur. Ethn.*, p. 47, fig. 12) illustrates two clusters of characteristic Hopi feathers copied by Mr. G. K. Gilbert from petroglyphs at Oakley Springs, Arizona. The first cluster belongs to the type shown in our fig. 57 as eagle tails, the second to that illustrated in fig. 31. They were identified by the Oraibi chief, Tuba, and so far as known have not been subsequently figured.

This type of feather sometimes forms a part of a bird's tail, but it does not occur in the wings, although, as above stated, it occurs under a wing or on the body or the head of a bird, a localization that leads to the belief that the device was designed to represent a breast feather, such as the Hopi now use in their prayers. In ancient Hopi symbolism it is often attached to circles representing the sun and represents a tail feather.

In plate 76, *a*, three feathers are represented with pointed tips and without interior markings. It is one of the simplest drawings of the type mentioned.

This figure illustrates a well-known type of feather symbol. It has many variations, all clearly differentiated from the form last described, from which it differs in its elongate form and pointed tip. What may be regarded as a subtype of this is marked with diagonal bands drawn either at right angles at one edge or extending across the figure and terminating at right angles to the opposite edge. Feather symbols of this type, which have not been identified with any particular bird, are constantly found in birds' tails and wings.

The next design (pl. 76, *b*) is similar in outline, but the three feathers are painted solid black and are separated by spaces. This conventional form of feather is common on wings and tails of birds.

The group of symbols shown in plate 76, *c*, has pointed tips, like the others described, but part of the shaft is painted, while the other is plain, the line of demarcation between which is drawn diagonally. This form occurs on the tails rather than on the wings of birds.

The tips of the feathers in plate 76, *d*, are connected by a black band and are divided by short vertical lines. A distinguishing feature of this symbol is the oblique marking of each feather on the right side, by which the feathers are narrowed at the base. A solid semicircular figure with a double notch ornaments the upper edge. The few known examples of this type of feather symbol are from the tails of unknown birds.

The next form of feather, shown in *e*, differs from the last in that the shaft is spotted and the proximal end is cut diagonally in a somewhat different way.[1] The tips are slit as in the figure last described.

The width of the feathers shown in *f* is uniform throughout. The distal ends are tipped with black; the proximal ends are each ornamented with a black triangle. Midway of the length of the feathers are four continuous parallel horizontal lines.

The two feathers shown in *g* have in one instance a black and in the other a white tip separated from the rest of the shaft by an oblique line. The essential difference between this form of pointed

---

[1] Compare feathers, pl. 90, *wf*.

VARIOUS FORMS OF CONVENTIONALIZED FEATHERS

feather and those previously considered is that the diagonal line marking the tip is drawn at a greater angle.

The six feathers shown in *h* resemble the last, but the terminal portions of three are spotted instead of solid black. Like some of the others described, this form tapers slightly from its distal end to its base.

In *i* the feathers are likewise pointed at their tips, but are of almost uniform breadth. Each is intersected by a series of triangles and parallel lines, and suspended from the latter, one in each feather, are several vertical lines, each with terminal dots.

The symbol shown in *j* is not unlike that already illustrated, but it has in addition to the structure enumerated a lateral hornlike appendage common in the tails of birds (see pl. 90, *i*, *tf*).

The form of feather design shown in *k* is somewhat different from those already considered. The distal end is broad and pointed; the proximal narrows almost to a point. The left half of the body of the feather is black; the remainder, including the point, is plain. The design *l* has the same general form as *k*, but its tip is marked in a different manner.

The double-pointed symbol represented in *m* was evidently designed as a feather (possibly two feathers), with parallel sides, and pointed tips painted black. The symbol *n* is similar to *d* in outline, but it lacks the terminal slit and black bands. There project, however, from the angles formed by the tips of the feathers three vertical lines, each with an arrow point at the extremity and two short crosslines, as in one of the bird designs previously described (fig. 35). The present design represents wing feathers; the complete bird figure (fig. 35), where they also occur, represents a thunderbird.

The three tail feathers shown in *o* are in no respect peculiar. The two-pointed appendages seen above are an almost constant feature of the drawings of birds as seen from the back. The feathers represented in *p* are unlike others in their mode of attachment and in the ornamentation at the base.

Thus far we have considered a type of feathers with pointed tips (pl. 76, *a–p*) imparting to the whole tail a serrate appearance. While in the next figure, *q*, the tail feathers still terminate in points, a black band connecting their extremities is prolonged at each side, recalling the tail of certain swallows.

Feathers are often represented on Sikyatki pottery as elsewhere in the Southwest by parallel straight lines. The feathers represented in *r* are exceptional in that their length varies considerably, the median feather here being the longest.

While undoubtedly the series of designs shown in *s* to *bb*, inclusive, in each instance representing the feathers in the tail of a bird, are all highly conventionalized, in one or two instances, as u and bb, the relation to feathers can be recognized only by comparative studies.

The design illustrated in cc, taken from the neck of a vase, represents several peculiar feathers of a type not yet described but highly characteristic. Comparison of this with that of dd shows the similarity of the two and suggests that they pertain to the same kind of bird. The tails represented in v, aa, and bb are characteristic; the last represents tail feathers hanging from the band later described.

The series of feathers (possibly tail feathers) shown in several figures have rounded tips, and as a rule are of uniform size and without ornamentation. In plate 77, a, the three feathers composing the tail are painted black and are slightly separated, while those of b are half black and half plain, the solid area being separated from the plain by a diagonal line extending from the proximal to the distal extremity.

The four feathers in c are separated by slight intervals and lightly shaded; otherwise they are similar to those in a. The two outside feathers of d are much broader than the middle feather, which is reduced to a narrow line. In e the three feathers are broader at the tips, in which respect they differ from c.

In the tail shown in f, the feathers are indicated by shallow notches from which short parallel lines extend inward. They are without superficial markings. Figure g belongs to the notched type represented above.

The four feather symbols shown in the drawing of the bird's tail illustrated in h differ from all others in the shape of their distal ends, which are alternately black and plain, and are without superficial ornamentation. Evidently this feather design, which is represented on a single vessel from Sikyatki, is of a distinct type.

There is some doubt whether i represents a bird's tail, the head and body from which the design was taken being more like those of a moth or a butterfly. The meaning of the design in j is also doubtful. Figure k represents a single "breath" feather like that shown in figure 57.

There is a general resemblance between the tail feathers of the bird designed in e and l; the latter represents the tail of a bird, hanging between two triangles under a star design.

Figure m represents a bird's tail with three tail feathers and lateral extensions, while in n, where we also have a figure of the tail of a bird, each feather is marked by a rectangular pattern. The four pairs of parallel lines extending from these feathers may be regarded as parts of these structures.

Figures o to q, while suggesting bird and feather designs, are still more or less problematical. In the same category belong the designs

CONVENTIONALIZED TAIL FEATHERS

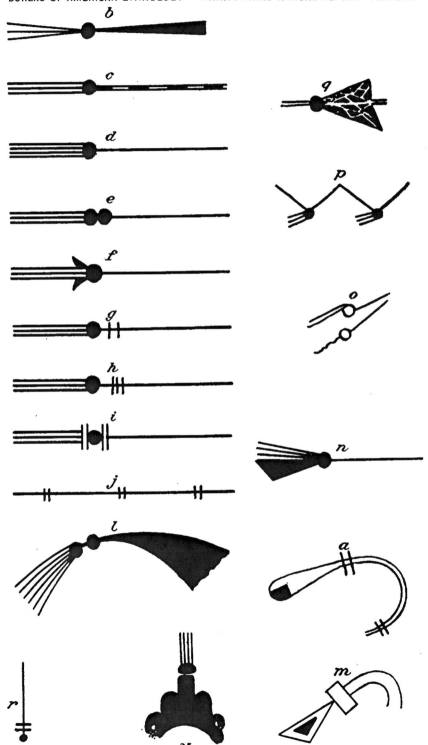

CONVENTIONALIZED FEATHERS ATTACHED TO STRINGS (NAKWAKWOCI)

illustrated in figures *r* to *u*. There is reason to believe that of these *o–r* represent feathers, but a definite identification can not yet be made of figures *s–u*.

Two triangular designs, one above another, are believed to represent feathers, but are rarely found on ancient Hopi pottery. They appear on the heads of birds in Acoma, Laguna, and other

FIG. 59.—Feathers.

pottery designs, which are the nearest modern representatives of ancient Hopi decorations.

FIG. 60.—Curved feathers.

A unique feather symbol from Sikyatki is characterized by a cigar-shaped body outlined at the distal end, which is plain (fig. 59).

There often occurs on Sikyatki pottery a combination of feather designs, generally three, with other symbols. One form of these (fig. 60) has four curved tail feathers. Other feathers of aberrant shape are shown in figure 61, *a–e*.

FEATHERS SUSPENDED FROM STRINGS

In their ceremonies the modern Hopi priests use in great numbers a kind of prayer offering called *nakwakwoci*, consisting of breast feathers tied in a prescribed way to the ends of strings. The same type of prayer offerings is one of the most common designs on Sikyatki pottery. Various modifications of it are shown in the accompanying illustration (fig. 62).

This use of the feather string as a decorative device is seemingly peculiar to prehistoric Hopi pottery, not having been found in the pictography of the people formerly inhabiting the valleys of San Juan and Little Colorado Rivers. This restriction in its use indicates its local

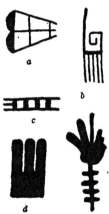

FIG. 61. — Conventional feathers.

origin and application, although descendants of clans from both the San Juan and the Little Colorado are represented among the Hopi.

FIG. 62.—Parallel lines representing feathers.

In one of the simplest forms of the stringed-feather designs is a line (pl. 78, *b*, *c*, *d*) sometimes taking the form of an elongate triangle, terminating in a ball from which spring three or more diverging or parallel lines. This enlargement on stringed-feather designs may represent a knot, as will appear from certain variations in the form of the feathered string to which attention will be given later.

In some cases (*e*, *l*) two knots appear between the string and the attached feathers, while in another instance (*f*) one of the knots or balls is replaced by two triangles.

Other representations of stringed-feather or *nakwakwoci* designs show modifications in each of the three elements mentioned, the line (string), the enlargement (knot), and the terminal projections (feathers). The occurrence of crossbars near the dot (*g*, *h*, *i*) vary in number from one to four, and are always parallel, but usually are placed on one side of the knot, although in some cases (*i*) they appear on both sides. In one example (*j*) no ball or knot is provided, the *nakwakwoci* consisting merely of the string intersected by pairs of equidistant crosslines. A special modification of the dot with crosslines is shown in the figure with the leaflike attachment (*q*).

One of the most significant of the stringed-feather designs is shown in *a*, where a feather of the first type is attached to the string intersected by crosslines. As a terminal element in corresponding designs is a typical feather symbol, this figure is also identical. The figure of a string with enlargements and a pair of lines (*g*) probably represents that form of stringed feather called by the Hopi a *purhu*, "road," an offering laid by the Hopi on the trails approaching the pueblo to indicate that ceremonies are being performed, or on altars · to show the pathway of blessings.

In another stringed-feather design (*n*) appears a triangular symbol attached to the enlargement, the string terminating in radiating lines. The feather sometimes preserves its triangular form (*m*). These variations in the drawings of stringed feathers and the modifications of the knot, string, and terminal attachments, are constantly repeated in Sikyatki pottery decoration.

SKY-BAND

Many food bowls from Sikyatki have a band from which is suspended the figure of a nondescript animal passing diametrically across it. Representations of a similar band with like appendage girt the necks of small pottery objects and are, so far as is known, characteristic of prehistoric Hopi pottery.

Lines identified as sky-bands shown in plate 79 vary from single (*a*) or double (*b*) to a broad undecorated band (*c*). In its simplest form the sky-band extends entirely across the inside of the bowl, but in the more complicated examples it surrounds the vessel parallel with the rim surrounding the design on the inside of the bowl. Appendages of several kinds as dots (*d*) or as stars (*f*), made up of oblong figures in terrace form placed at intervals, are attached

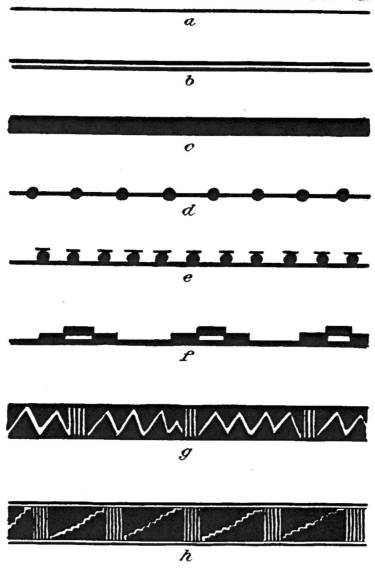

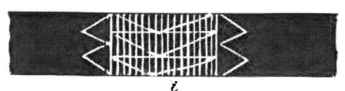

i

SKY-BANDS

to this band. The sky-band itself varies in width, being broad or narrow, crossed by series of vertical parallel, zigzag, or other lines arranged at intervals, or alternating with geometrical figures (g, h). In a single example (i) the decoration is etched into the burnt clay, although in most instances the decorations are painted.

Various explanations of the meaning of this band have been suggested, it being regarded by some of the priests as the Milky Way, by others as the path of the sun through the sky, but so far as known this ancient design is rare on modern Hopi ware.[1] According to Harrington the Tewa recognize a "backbone" of the sky.

In several Hopi legends there are allusions to a monster bird that had been killed and hung in the sky by a cultus hero; and the general character of this decorative band in Sikyatki pottery decoration renders it probable that it was intended to represent some supernatural being, as the Sky god.

The chief interest of the Sikyatki sky-band lies in the figure or figures attached to it, or suspended from it, and regarded as the conventionalized representation of a bird. Sometimes the creature is placed longitudinally, sometimes vertically. In some instances it is elaborately drawn, in others it is a simple geometric figure bearing so little resemblance to a life form as to make it one of the most highly conventionalized of all ancient Hopi designs.

Like other bird designs, these suspended figures may be considered under two heads: (1) Those attached to the band in such a way as to be seen from above (the dorsal side) or from below (the ventral side); and (2) those suspended lengthwise of the band, showing one side in which the tail and other parts are twisted into a plane at right angles. The structure and relations of the hanging figure can best be seen by holding the bowl in such manner that the sky-band is horizontal, bringing the body of the suspended animal into the lower semicircle.   •

VERTICAL ATTACHMENT TO SKY-BAND

Several Sikyatki pottery designs showing the sky-band with the bird figure hanging vertically from it are shown in the accompanying illustrations. In order that the modifications in form may be readily followed, those parts of the bird figures regarded as homologous are indicated by the same letters.

---

[1] The only design in modern Hopi symbolism comparable with the sky-band occurs on a wooden slab on the altar of the Owakulti, a society priestess whose ancestors are said to have formerly lived at the historic pueblo of Awatobi. This slab is attached to the uprights of an altar, by means of flat slabs of wood, some arranged vertically, others horizontally. On it is depicted, among other symbolic figures, a representation of a bird.

The design in figure 63 represents one of the simplest forms of bird symbols. A hornlike appendage is attached to the sky-band, on each side of an elongate vertical body from which depends a

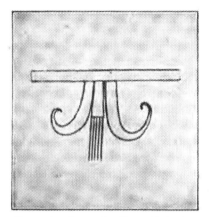

FIG. 63.—Conventionalized bird form hanging from sky-band; top view.

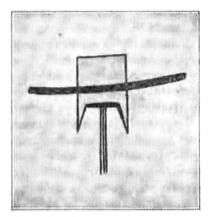

FIG. 64.—Conventionalized bird form hanging from sky-band; top view.

number of parallel lines representing tail feathers. The identification of this design as that of a bird is based on comparative studies of designs less conventional in character, to which attention has been and will later be called.

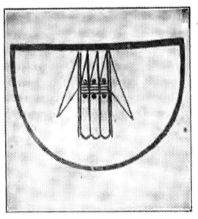

FIG. 65.—Conventionalized bird form hanging from sky-band; top view.

FIG. 66.—Conventionalized bird form hanging from sky-band; top view.

A modification of the pendent body on the sky-band[1] appears to have introduced the new element shown in figure 64 in which the body is drawn. Although considerable variation exists in the form of the other parts, a morphological identity exists in all these figures. In figure 65, in which the feathers differ somewhat from those of the

---

[1] The author has seen in the American Museum of Natural History, New York, a single specimen of doubtful provenance, bearing a similar design.

last design, the parallel lines representing the bird's tail are really seen. The design shown in figure 66 is still more elaborate than the last, especially in the anterior semicircle,[1] opposite that in which the tail feathers are depicted.

Fɪɢ. 67. — Conventionalized bird form hanging from sky-band; top view.

Fɪɢ. 68.—Conventionalized bird form hanging from sky-band; top view.

The portion of the design situated in the anterior semicircle of figure 67 has no resemblance to a bird's head, being destitute of eyes or beak. The backward extending appendages on each side of the tail and the tail itself has a projection on each side.

Fɪɢ. 69.—Conventionalized bird form hanging from sky-band; top view.

In figure 68 the whole anterior part of the design above the sky-band is colored, the head appearing as a still darker semicircle. The tail feathers are here reduced to simple parallel lines. The general form of figure 69 is birdlike, but its affinity to the bird figures, pendent from a sky-band, is closer than to any others. The homologous parts—tail feathers, lateral body extensions, sky-band, and head—may be readily recognized; the last mentioned is an ornamented rectangle. The whole anterior hemisphere of this design is occupied by representations of feathers arranged in two clusters, while in the surrounding area their triple lines are crossed similarly to that occurring in other hanging bird figures. It is but a step from this figure to the group of unattached bird designs already considered.

---

[1] For convenience this may be designated the anterior in distinction to that on the other side of the sky-band which may be termed the posterior semicircle.

The wings of figure 70 are outspread and the head consists of two terraced bodies conventionally placed. The body and the tail of this figure are not exceptional, but dragon flies are also represented.

Figure 71 presents a conventionalized bird seen in profile, and a broad sky-band to which are attached representations of feathers and other organs suggesting a bird.

An animal depicted in figure 72 is one of three similar figures from the neck of the same vase, which are connected by a line or band. The design shown in figure 73 repre-

FIG. 70.—Conventionalized bird form hanging from sky-band; top view.

sents a highly conventionalized bird hanging from the sky-band with head and wings on one side and tail feathers below.

BIRDS ATTACHED LONGITUDINALLY TO SKY-BAND

The designs shown in figure 74 represent the simplest forms of birds attached lengthwise to the sky-band. The parallel lines on the left hand of the observer are supposed to represent tail feathers and the curve on the right, the heads, or possibly the wings.

One of the best designs representing a bird attached to a sky-band is shown in figure 75, taken from a bowl in the Wattron collection now owned by the Field Columbian Museum, of Chicago. The interior surface of this bowl is considerably worn by use, and the figure a little indistinct, but the

FIG. 71.—Conventionalized bird form hanging from sky-band; top view.

extremities of a band appear. There is a fairly realistic figure on each side of a bird with head and wings above and tail below a

diametrical band. There are zigzag markings, supposed to represent lightning, on the under side of the wing. The tail is spread
out amply enough to show the different feathers which compose it;
and at the bases or on its under side corresponding in position with
like symbols on the wing there appear two zigzag figures. The
significance of two curved bodies
hanging from the sky-band, one
on each side of the tail of this

FIG. 78. — Conventionalised bird
form hanging from sky-band;
top view.

FIG. 72. — Conventionalised bird form
hanging from sky-band; top view

figure, can not be satisfactorily interpreted, but the bird design shown
in figure 76 has four tail feathers, a prolongation on the opposite side
representing a head, and a curved extension comparable with a wing
in other figures. The so-called
wing terminates in a triangular
feather.

The two designs, figures 76 and
77, have parts which evidently
correspond, the latter being one
of the most beautiful in the collection. Both represent from the
side an unknown bird hanging
from a band extending across the
middle of the bowls. Although
the details of organs are more
carefully depicted in the latter,
there can hardly be a doubt that
similar animals were intended in
both designs.

It requires some imagination
to discover a conventionalized
bird in figure 78, but we may

FIG. 74.—Lateral view of bird hanging
from sky-band.

regard it as such. We have in this figure a good example of a change
in outline that may be produced by duplication or by representing
both sides of the body or its organs and appendanges in the same

place. Three tail feathers are here apparent; the body is square, with zigzag white lines, and the head, here twisted into a vertical position, has a triangular form. The two crescentic appendages, one on

the right side, the other on the left, represent halves of wings which are theoretically supposed to have been slit longitudinally and folded backward[1] in order that both sides may be shown on the same plane; the two bodies arising from the concave edges of these crescents—one to the left, the other to the right of the s q u a r e b o d y—represent legs. Their unusual form is brought about by a twisting of body and tail, by which feathers of the latter are brought to longitudinal

FIG. 75.—Lateral view of bird hanging from sky-band.

position, and one of the legs is twisted to the right side and the other to the left. If the two appendages supposed to represent the legs or the two parts shaped like crescentlike knives were brought together, the two crescents would likewise merge into one, and we would then have a highly conventionalized bird with three tail feathers and a triangular head, the body being represented by a square design crossed diagonally by zigzag figures each in its own rectangular inclosed field.

DECORATIONS ON EXTERIORS OF FOOD BOWLS

The exterior surface of almost every bowl from Sikyatki is decorated with lines or geometrical designs. Many of these designs may represent animals, probably birds highly conventionalized or so aberrant that the avian form can be recognized only by comparative or morphological studies. They are confined to one side of the bowl; there appears to be little resem-

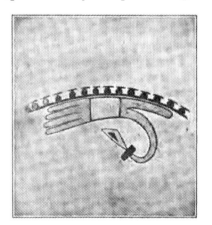

FIG. 76.—Lateral view of bird with extended wing.

blance and no connection between them and the figure depicted on the inside of the same bowls. Although linear in form, one end is sometimes so crooked or bent at an angle, not curved, as to form a head, while the other bears parallel lines, representations of the tail feathers, terraces, or triangles.

---

[1] See also *Seventeenth Ann. Rept. Bur. Amer. Ethn.*, pl. CL, *a*, and CXLVI, *d*.

In plate 80, a, we have a characteristic example of one of these exterior decorations. The crooked end is supposed to represent a bird's head; to the other end, or tail, are appended six feathers like those already considered. A row of five stars is strung along the band. A likeness to a bird is very obscure in b, while c shows several simple triangles with stepped figures in the middle and triangles at the ends. Design d has a square form and two triangles appended to each opposite angle. The appendages on the remaining opposite angles have four parallel lines. Design e consists of two highly conventionalized bird symbols, united to a third which forms the interior design.

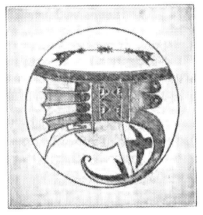

Fig. 77.—Lateral view of bird hanging from sky-band.

The design f recalls the sky-band described in the preceding pages. The extremities of this so-called band are enlarged into round spots from which arise parallel lines and triangular designs. From it hang terraced and crooked figures, while strung along one side at equal intervals are five stars, a common accompaniment of sky symbols. The bird symbol comes out clearly in g, where the crook design with terraces is repeated.

Fig. 78.—Lateral view of bird hanging from sky-band.

All crooked figures have a similarity in general form, some more closely resembling birds than others, and it is taken for granted that the intention of the artist was to represent a bird in plate 81, a, notwithstanding the avian form is highly conventionalized. Design b is composite, consisting of a rectangular figure, to the angles of which are attached feathers. Terraced and triangular figures of unknown significance, stars, and other designs cover the rectangle. Design c is made up of a triangle with notched borders and a central rectangle, with a dot characterizes this design; it has also two triangular extensions that may represent feathers. Design *d* resembles previous figures identified as feathers and terraces hanging from a sky-band.

The most prominent part of the design *e* is a crook and parallel lines. In *f* are variously combined triangles with appended feathers, crooks, and terraced designs, so united as to make up a compound decoration of geometric character.

The geometrical designs in the series, plate 82, *a–f*, may be interpreted as representing birds in flight or with extended wings. Considered in this way, it appears that we have in the figure on each side a highly conventionalized wing forming triangles with extensions at one angle, ending in terraces, crooks, or other designs. In these figures we constantly have a line that may be likened to the sky-band, each end generally terminating in a dot to which parallel lines are attached.

Design *a* has two triangular bodies resembling the letter W, and the line terminating in two dots has two crossbars, while in *b* there is a union of designs. Elongated triangles terminate in lines which are enlarged into dots. These triangles are modified on one side into crooks with smaller triangles.

From remote resemblances rather than similarity of form, *c* is placed near the preceding. Here a band is enlarged at the end representing the knots with attached parallel lines or feathers. The triangular pendants of *b* and the line with terminal dots of *a* are here represented. On the middle vertical of this figure is a trapezoidal design with notched edges.

The elements of *d* form a compound in which triangles predominate. Two W-shaped designs, *e* and *f*, have a form quite unlike *a*, *b*, *c*, and *d*. Of these, *f* is the more complicated, but the similarity of the two is apparent.

Plate 83, *a*, represents two triangles with serrate margins hanging to a horizontal band, one end of which terminates in dots and lines, the other with two parallel notched feathers.

Plate 84, *a–c*, have the W shape shown in plate 82, *e*, *f;* the approach to the conventional bird form with extended wings and tail being most marked in *a*. Design *d* on plate 84 recalls plate 83, *f*, with modifications that are apparent.

The above-mentioned geometrical figures from the exteriors of Sikyatki food bowls show considerable variety of form but all can be reduced to a few elemental designs throughout in which the curved line is absent. The rectangular design is always dominant, but it will be seen from the following plate that it is not omnipresent, especially on the interiors of bowls.

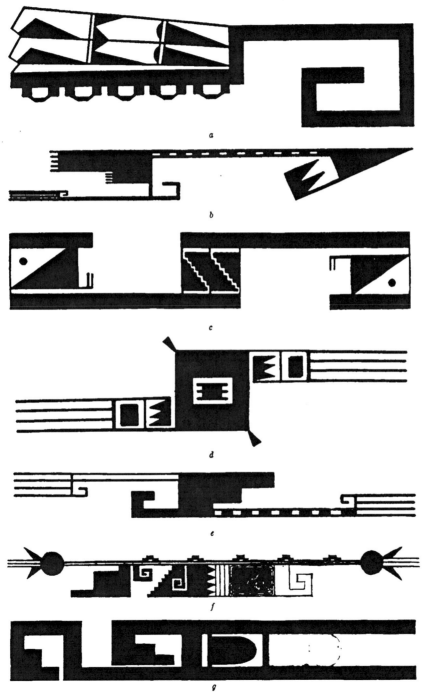

GEOMETRICAL FIGURES ON OUTSIDE OF BOWLS

CONVENTIONALIZED BIRD DESIGNS

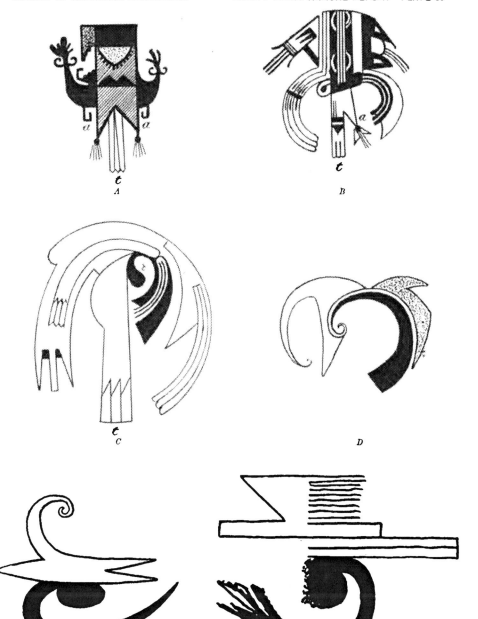

CONVENTIONALIZED BIRD DESIGNS

Curved Figure with Attached Feathers

The curved spiral figures shown in plates 85 and 86 are combinations of simple and complicated designs, among the most conspicuous of which are feathers. When these figures are placed in the same position it is possible to recognize three or four components which are designated (a) spiral, (b) appendage to the tip of the spiral, (c) a bundle of feathers recalling a bird's tail, and (d) and (e) other parts of unknown homology occasionally represented. In plate 85, A the appendage b to the spiral a is two triangles and two supplemental spirals arising from their attachments. There is no representation of c, d, or e in this figure.

In B of the same plate the elements a, b, c, and d are represented. The appendage b attached to the tip of the spiral a has the form of a feather of the first type (see pl. 76), and four parallel lines, c, indicating feathers, are attached to the body. The two toothlike appendages e, of unknown significance, complete the figure. In plate 85, C, the design a has two dots b on the distal tip, from one of which arises a number of lines. The fact that b in figure B is a feather leads to the belief that b in figure C is the same design.

Plate 85, D and E, have a resemblance in form, a and c being represented in both; b and e are wanting in E. The different elements in these designs can be readily seen by comparing the same lettering in F and G, and in plate 86, A and B, where a new element, t, is introduced.

Plate 86, B and E, are highly conventionalized designs; they suggest bird form, examples of which have been already considered elsewhere, but are very much modified.

There can be no doubt that it was intended to represent birds or parts of birds as feathers in many of the above figures, but the perspective is so distorted that their morphology or relative position on the bird to which they belong can not be made out. In plate 86, A, for instance, the bird's body seems to be split in two parts and laid on a flat plane. The pendent body, t, in the middle would be a representation of a bird's tail composed of three feathers and with a double triangle terminating in dots from which arise lines of would-be feathers.

Two of the parts, a and t, that occur in the last mentioned, are found in plate 86, B, in somewhat modified form. Thus the position of the tail feathers, t, figure C, is taken by feathers of a different form, their extremities being cut off flat and not curved. The bundles of feathers in B and C are here reversed, the left side of B corresponding to the right of C, and the appendage on the left of the tail of *B* being represented by the appendage on the right of *C*. There are other remote likenesses between them.

SPIDER AND INSECTS

Other flying animals, like bats and insects, are depicted on Sikyatki pottery, but not as constantly as birds. The spider, and insects like the dragon fly, moth, and butterfly, are the most common. In Hopi mythology the spider[1] and the sun are associated, the former being the symbol of an earth goddess. Although no design that can be referred to the spider has yet been found on Sikyatki pottery, it is not wanting from Hopi (pl. 87, *c*).

The symbol of the dragon fly, which occurs on several bowls from ancient Hopi ruins, is a line often enlarged at one end to form a head, and always with two crossbars near this enlargement to indicate wings. As this insect lives near springs and is constantly associated in modern symbolism with water it is probable that its occurrence on ancient Hopi pottery has practically the same significance as in modern conceptions.

BUTTERFLY AND MOTH

Five typical figures that may be referred to the butterfly or moth occur on Sikyatki pottery. These figures have in common a triangular body which suggests a highly conventionalized picture of a bird. Their wings are, as a rule, extended horizontally, assuming the attitude of moths while at rest, there being only one of the five examples where wings are folded above the back, the normal position of these organs in a butterfly. With one exception, all these conventional butterfly figures bear two curved rows of dots on the head, probably intended to represent antennæ.

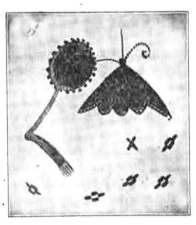

FIG. 79.—Butterfly and flower.

The figure of a moth in figure 79 has a body of triangular form, and the extremities of the wings are shown on each side of a medially placed backward-extending projection, which is the posterior end

---

[1] The Kokyan, or Spider, clan is not made much of in Hopi legends gathered at Walpi, but Kokyanwügti, the Spider woman, is an important supernatural in the earliest mythologies, especially those of the Snake people. She was the mentor of the Snake youth in his journey to the underworld and an offering at her shrine is made in the Oraibi Snake dance. The picture of the spider with that of the sun suggests that the Spider woman is a form of the earth goddess. No personation of Spider woman has been seen by the author in the various ceremonies he has witnessed.

of the abdomen. These wings bear white dots on their posterior edges suggesting the markings on certain genera of butterflies.[1] There arises from the head, which here is circular, a single jointed appendage curved at the end, possibly the antenna, and an unjointed appendage, like a proboscis, inserted into a figure of a flower, mounted on a stalk that terminates at the other extremity in five parallel extensions or roots. A row of dots about the periphery of the flower suggests petals. The figures are accompanied by crosses representing stars.

Fɪɢ. 80.—Butterfly with extended proboscis.

The second moth design (fig. 80) has even a closer resemblance to a bird than the last, for it also has a single antenna or row of dots connected by a curved line. It likewise has several curved lines resembling a crest of feathers on top of the head, and lines recalling the tail of a bird. The head this figure bears is a cross suggesting a female butterfly or moth.[2]

Fɪɢ. 81.—Highly conventionalized butterfly.

The body in figure 81 is crossed by five lines converging at one angle, imparting to it the appearance of having been formed by a union of several spherical triangles on each of which appear rectangular spaces painted black. A head is not differentiated from the body, but at the point of union of the five lines above mentioned there arise two rows of dots which have the form of circles, each inclosing a dot. From analogy these are supposed to represent antennæ. The middle of wing-shaped extensions recalling butterfly designs are marked by circular figures in figure 82, but the absence in this figure of a head with jointed appendages renders it doubtful whether it represents an insect. The shape of the body and its

---

[1] Except that the head bears a jointed antenna this figure might be identified as a bird, the long extension representing the bird's bill.

[2] The figures of serpents on the sand mosaic of the Antelope altar at Walpi bear similar crosses or diagonals, crossing each other at right angles. The Antelope priests interpret this marking as a sign of the female.

appendages resembling feathers indicate, so far as they go, that
this design represents some bird.

It will be noted that in one of the above-mentioned figures, identified as a moth, flowers are indicated by dotted circles, while in another similar circle, figures, also surrounded with dots, are represented on the wings. One pair
of wings is represented in the last-
mentioned figure, but a second
pair placed behind the larger may
have been confounded with the
tail feathers. In one of these figures from Sikyatki there is a row
of dots around the margin of the
wings—a common but not universal feature in modern pictures of
butterfly figures. None of the
butterfly figures have representations of legs, which is not strange
considering how inconspicuous
these appendages are among these
insects.

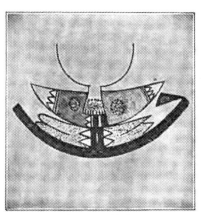

FIG. 82.—Moth.

A most striking figure of a butterfly is represented by six drawings
on the so-called "butterfly vase" (fig. 83). These, like the above-
mentioned, resemble birds, but they all have antennæ, which identify
them as insects. These six figures (pl. 90) are supposed to be connected with the six cardinal points which in modern Hopi belief have
sex—the butterfly corresponding to the north, male; to the west,
female; to the south, male; to the
east, female; to the above, male;
and to the below, female. The
wings of all these insects are represented as extended, the anterior
pair extending far beyond the
posterior, while both have a uniform color and are without marginal dots. The appendages to
the head are two curved rows of
dots representing antennæ, and
two parallel lines are the mouth
parts or possibly the proboscis.
The markings on the bodies and
the terminal parallel lines are like

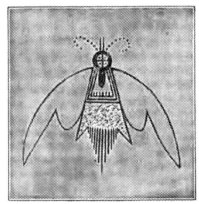

FIG. 83.—Moth.

tail feathers of birds. The heads of three figures, instead of having
diagonal lines, are covered with a crosshatching, *b*, *b*, *b*, and are
supposed to represent the males, as the former, *a*, *a*, *a*, are females.[1]

---

[1] Rain, lightning, animals, plants, sky, and earth, in the modern Hopi conception, are
supposed to have sex.

A moth with a conventionalized geometric form is represented in figure 84 with outstretched wings, a rounded abdomen, and a spotted rectangular body recalling designs on the upper embroidered margin of modern ceremonial blankets. A like figure has been elsewhere described by the author as a butterfly.[1] It occurs on the stone slab which once formed one side of an Awatobi altar.[2] We

Fɪɢ. 84.—Moth or geometrical form.

have more complicated forms of butterflies represented in figures 85–87, the identification of which is even more doubtful than the last. Figure 86 reproduces in its several parts figure 85, being composed of a central design, around which are arranged six triangles, one of the last being placed above, another below, the main figure, and there are two on each side. The design, figure 88, is circular, the alternately colored quadrants forming two hourglass combinations. The double triangle, shown in figure 84, resembles a butterfly symbol, having a close likeness to a figure of this insect found on the Awatobi tablet above mentioned. This figure also resembles triangular designs painted on the walls of modern Hopi rooms and in cliff-dwellings (Cliff Palace). These figures present very remote likenesses to butterfly symbols and their identification as such is difficult.

Fɪɢ. 85.—Geometrical form of moth.

Fɪɢ. 86.—Highly conventionalized butterfly.

Fɪɢ. 87.—Geometrical form of moth.

GEOMETRICAL DESIGNS

The geometrical designs on the pottery from Sikyatki consist of two well-recognized groups: (1) Purely ornamental or nonsymbolic geometrical figures, and (2) highly conventional life forms. Some of the figures of the second group may be geometrical representations of birds or other animals; but the former are simply embellishments used to beautify the objects on which they are painted. Purely decorative designs, not being symbolic, will not be specially considered, as they do not come within the scope of the present treatise. An interpretation of the significance of many of the second group of geometrical designs is not possible, although they probably represent animal forms.

Fɪɢ. 88. — Circle with triangles.

[1] The Butterfly in Hopi Myth and Ritual, fig. 61, *f*.
[2] Ibid., p. 586.

The strictly geometrical figures so frequently found on pottery from Sikyatki recall the linear decorations almost universal in ancient southwestern ware.

No one who has carefully compared specimens of decorated pottery from Sikyatki with examples from any other southwestern region could fail to be impressed with the differences in some of the geometrical designs from the two localities. Such designs on the Sikyatki ware are almost always rectangular, rarely curved. As compared with pottery from cliff-dwellings there is a paucity or entire absence of terraced designs in the ancient Hopi ware, while zigzags representing lightning are comparatively rare. The characteristic geometrical decorations on Sikyatki pottery are found on the outside of the food bowls, in which respect they are notably different from those of other ceramic areas. Designs on Sikyatki pottery show few survivals of preexisting materials or evolution from transfer of those on textiles of any kind. Such as do exist are so masked that they shed little light on current theories of art evolution.

The designs on ancient Hopi pottery are in the main mythological, hence their true interpretation involves a knowledge of the religious ideas and especially of such psychological elements as sympathetic magic, so prevalent among the Hopi of to-day. The idea that by the use of symbols man could influence supernatural beings was no doubt latent in the mind of the potter and explains the character of the symbols in many instances. The fact that the bowls on which these designs are painted were found with the dead, and contained food for the departed, implies a cult of the dead, or at least a belief in a future life.

RAIN CLOUDS

The most constant geometric designs on Pueblo pottery are those representing the rain cloud, and from analogy we would expect to find the rain-cloud figures conspicuously on ancient Hopi pottery. We look in vain on Sikyatki ware for the familiar semicircular symbols of rain clouds so constant among the modern Hopi; nor do we find the rectangular terraced form which is equally common. These modifications were probably lately introduced into Hopiland by those colonists of alien clans who came after the destruction of Sikyatki, and consequently are not to be expected on its pottery. Their place was taken by other characteristitc forms closely allied to rectangular terraced figures from which hang parallel lines, representing falling rain in modern symbolism.[1] The typical Sikyatki rain-cloud symbol is terraced without rain symbols and finds its nearest relative on pottery derived from the eastern pueblo region.

[1] Introduced into the Hopi pueblos by colonists from the Rio Grande; its most conspicuous variant can be seen on the tablets worn in a masked dance called Humis (Jemez) Kachina.

The form of rain-cloud symbol on Sikyatki pottery may be regarded as characteristic of the Kokop clan which, according to legends, settled this ancient pueblo. Modified variants of this form of rain-cloud symbol occur on almost every specimen in the Sikyatki collection, and can be seen hanging from "sky-bands" with appended star signs or without such connections.

The most common Sikyatki symbol of a rain cloud is shown in figure 89 and plate 90, *f, g*. These rain-cloud designs rarely occur singly, being more often six in number, as if intended to represent the six cardinal points recognized in Hopi ceremonies. We find the Sikyatki rain-cloud symbols resembling somewhat those of the modern Zuñi, or figures of clouds found on the characteristic designs on Little

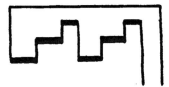

Fɪɢ. 89.—Rain cloud.

Colorado ceramics. Somewhat similar angular terraced forms are almost universally used in eastern pueblos as rain-cloud symbols, but the semicircular forms (fig. 90) of modern Hopi ceremonials, being apparently a highly specialized modification, rarely occur on Sikyatki pottery.

Stars

The star sign occurs as an equal armed cross formed by the approximation of four squares, leaving a central uncolored area. It is generally accompanied by a rain-cloud symbol or bird figures, although likewise found without them. We often find one arm of the component arms of the cross missing and two of the remaining arms adherent to a band; often these crosses have a circular enlargement at the junction of their arms. A simple equal armed cross is the sole decoration on the interior

Fɪɢ. 90.—Rain cloud.

of numerous food bowls, and there are several examples of St. Andrew's crosses, the triangular arms. of which have been interpreted as representing four conventionalized birds; no example of a cross with unequal arms has yet been found on Sikyatki pottery.

These crosses, like that with four arms representing the Sky god in modern Hopi symbolism, probably represent the Heart of the Sky. A similar cross is figured on paraphernalia used in modern Hopi rites or on altar slabs; when it is represented by a wooden frame, it is called *tokpela*, and hangs before the altar. The same object is. sometimes attached horizontally to the top of the helmet of the personification of the Sky god.[1]   The swastika is rare in ancient pottery and was not found at Sikyatki, although a single example was dug up at Awatobi and a few others were obtained from the Little Colorado ruins.

A multiple cross, formed of three parallel lines crossing three others at an angle, generally accompanies certain conventionalized figures of birds and in one example there are two multiple crosses, one on one side and one on another of a moth or butterfly symbol. The multiple cross is supposed to represent six canes used in a game, and on a prehistoric decorated bowl from ancient Shongopovi,[2] we find what appears to be a highly conventionalized bird figure occupying one-half of the interior of the bowl, while four figures representing these canes appear on the other. The bird figure, in this instance, is interpreted as a gambler's god, or a representation of the god of chance.

Sun Emblems

The most conventionalized sun emblem is a circle or ring with attached feathers. The Sikyatki design (pl. 87, b) is a circle bearing on its periphery appendages believed to represent feathers,

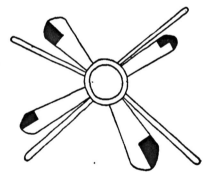

with accompanying lines, generally painted red, to represent the rays of the sun.[3]

The identification of the bird whose feathers are used in sun emblems has not yet been made, although the position of similar feathers on the body of other bird designs suggests that they represent eagle feathers. The feather of the eagle is commonly associated with both ancient and modern pictures representing the sun. Thus we have on a vessel from

FIG. 91.—Ring with appended feathers.

Sikyatki in figure 91 a design bearing four feathers arranged at intervals a quadrant apart alternating with radiating lines. If we interpret this figure in the light of modern symbolism the circle

---

[1] One symbol of the Sky god has the form of a Lightning god. It has a single curved horn on the head, lightning symbols on the legs, and carries a wooden framework in one hand and a bull-roarer in the other.

[2] *Twenty-second Ann. Rept. Bur. Ethn.*, pt. 1, fig. 74.

[3] In modern Hopi symbolism the sun is a disk with representations of eagle feathers around the periphery and radial lines at each quadrant, symbolic of the sun's rays. In disks worn on the back where real feathers are used the radial lines, or the sun's rays, are represented by horsehair stained red. In ceremonials the Sky god is personated by a bird whose figure occurs on Sikyatki pottery.

a

b

c

a

b

would be regarded as the sun and the feathers would be identified as eagle feathers, while the lines might be considered to represent the red rays of the four cardinal points.

In a bowl found at old Shongo-
povi, a ruin inhabited at the same epoch as Sikyatki, the sun takes the form of a sky bird. In this design the ring figure is replaced by a bird with wings, tail, and a beak, evidently the sun bird, hawk, or eagle (pl. 88, a).

Fɪɢ. 92.—Two circles with figure.

A theoretical interpretation of plate 88, b, is facilitated by a comparison of it with the design painted on a bowl from the Wattron collection, now in the Field Columbian Museum. As this has all the parts represented in figure 75, the conclusion would naturally be that the intention of the artist was to represent a bird figure.

Ring or circle shaped figures are found on several bowls from Sikyatki, and in one case (fig. 92) we find two circles side by side separated by a rectangular figure. The meaning of these rings and the accompanying design is not known.

Fɪɢ. 93.—Sun with feathers.

Concentric circles diametrically accompanied with two figures, one with a head and two lateral feathers, the other with the form of a hash-knife figure, are shown in figure 93.

In figure 94 the appendages of the ring design or sun emblem is much more complicated than any of the preceding. Each of the four quadrants has two appendages, a cluster with two feathers, and a curved body with a sickle-shaped extension, the whole giving a swastika-like appearance to the design. The interior of the circle is

Fɪɢ. 94.—Sun symbol.

likewise complicated, showing a structure difficult to interpret. From comparisons with preceding figures this is likewise regarded as a sun emblem.[1]

---

[1] In the Hopi ceremony, Powatawu, as performed at Oraibi, a picture representing the sun composed of a number of concentric circles of four different colors is made of sand on the kiva floor.

The ring or circle shown in figure 95 hangs from a band that may be likened to the sky-band of previous description.[1] A tri-

angle[2] is attached to the upper side of this band, while appended to the ring itself there is a featherlike object corresponding to a bird's tail and wing. This figure is unique in the Sikyatki collection of ancient Hopi pictography.

In figure 96 we find a leg appended to the lower side of the ring balanced by three wing feathers above or on the oppo-

FIG. 95. — Ring with appended feathers.

site side, two curved or crescentic extensions projecting from the rear, diametrically opposite which arises a curved body (head) with terminating sickle-shaped prolongation. This figure may be considered a bird design, having the tail twisted from a

FIG. 96.—Ring figure with legs and appended feathers.

lateral to a vertical position and the wing raised from the body.

In figure 97 we find a similar ring still further modified, the appendages to it being somewhat different. The ring is here broader than the last, inclosing an area crossed by two lines forming a cross, with short parallel lines at the ends of each arm. There is a head showing a circular face with dots indicating eyes and mouth. The head bears a crest of feathers between two horns. Here we have in place of the appendage to the lower side an elongated curved projection extending to the left, balanced by a short, stumpy, curved appendage on the right, while between these appendages hang four parallel lines

FIG. 97.—Sun emblem with appended feathers.

suggesting the highly conventional feathers of a tail. The horns with the crest of feathers between them recall the crest of the Sun

---

[1] If we interpret the sky-band as the path of the sun in the zenith the solar emblem hanging to it is significant.

[2] Some of the significant sun masks used by the Hopi have the mouth indicated by a triangle, others by hourglass designs.

god, of the Kachina clan, called Tunwup, a Sky god who flogs the children of modern Walpi.

The ring design in figure 98 has a bunch of three feathers in each quadrant, recalling the feathers of a sun emblem so well shown with other kinds of feathers in plate 76, *b*.

In figure 99 we have a circle with four appended bifurcated geometrical extensions projecting outward on the periphery, and recalling featherless tails of birds. This is also a highly conventionalized sun emblem reduced to a geometrical figure.

In connection with all these circular figures may be considered that shown in figure 92, the form of which is highly suggestive.

Fɪɢ. 98.—Sun symbol.

In the various modifications above mentioned we detect two elements, the ring and its peripheral appendages, interpreted as feathers, head, feet, and other bird organs. Sometimes the ring predominates, sometimes the feathers, and sometimes a bird figure replaces all, the ring being lost or reduced in size. This variation is primitive and quite consistent with the Pueblo conceptions and analogies known to occur in Hopi ceremonial paraphernalia. This variation illustrates what is elsewhere said about the influence of the magic power on the pictorial art of Hopi.[1]

The sun, to the Hopi mind, is likewise represented by a bird, or a compound of both becomes a Sky-god emblem; the horned serpent is the servant of the Sky god.

Fɪɢ. 99.—Sun symbol.

We find among the modern Hopi several disks with markings and decorations of such a character that they are identified as representations of the sun. One of these is worn by the leader of the kachinas in a ceremony called the Powamû, an elaborate rite, the purpose of which is to purify from evil influences. This Sun god[2]

---

[1] Pictures made by prehistoric man embody, first, when possible, the power of the animal or thing represented, or its essential characteristics; and second, the realistic form, shape, or outline.

[2] Several Hopi clans celebrate in a slightly different way the return of their Sun god, which is known by different names among them. The return of the Sun god of the Kachina clan at Walpi, commonly called Ahül, is elsewhere described. Shalako, the Sun god of the Patki clans, was derived from the Little Colorado region, the same source from which the Zuñi obtained their personage of the same name. His return is celebrated on the East Mesa of the Hopi at Sichomovi, the "Zuñi pueblo among the Hopi." Pautiwa is a Sun god of Zuñi clans at Sichomovi and is personated as at Zuñi pueblo. Kwataka, or the Sun god whose return is celebrated at Walpi in the winter solstice, Soyaluna, is associated with the great plumed serpent, a personation derived from the peoples of the Gila or some other river who practice irrigation. Eototo is a Sikyatki Sun god, derived from near Jemez, and is celebrated by Keres colonists.

is called Ahül, and the symbolism of his mask, especially feathers attached to the head, suggests some of the Sikyatki designs considered above.

RECTANGULAR FIGURES REPRESENTING SHRINES

The word *pahoki*, prayer-stick house or " shrine," is applied by the modern Hopi to the receptacle, commonly a ring of stones, in which prayer offerings are deposited, and receives its name from the special supernatural personage worshiped. These shrines are regarded as sacred by the Hopi and are particularly numerous in the neighborhood of the Hopi mesas.[1] They are ordinarily simply rude inclosures made of stones or flat stone slabs set on edge, forming boxes, which may either be closed or open on one side. The simplest pictographic representation of such a shrine is the same as that of a house, or a circular or rectangular figure. A similar design is drawn in meal on the floor of the kiva or traced with the same material on the open plaza when the priest wishes to represent a house or shrine. Elaborate pictures made of different colored sands to represent gods are often inclosed by encircling lines, the whole called a house of the gods. Thus the sand picture on the Antelope altar of the Snake dance is called the house of the rain-cloud beings.[2] When reptiles are washed on the ninth day of the Snake dance they are said to be thrown into the house, a sand picture of the mountain lion. It is customary to make in some ceremonies not only a picture of the god worshiped, but also a representation of his or her house. The custom of adding a picture of a shrine to that of the supernatural can be seen by examining a series of pictures of Hopi kachinas. Here the shrine is a rain-cloud symbol introduced to show that the house of the kachina represented is a rain cloud.

Sikyatki bowls decorated with figures identified as supernaturals often bear accompanying designs which may, from comparative reasoning, be interpreted as shrines of the supernatural being depicted. They have at times a form not unlike that of certain sand pictures, as in the case of the curved figure accompanying a highly conventionalized plumed serpent. A great variety of figures of this kind are found on Sikyatki bowls,[3] and often instead of being a rectangular figure they may be elongated more like a prayer offering.

The rectangular figure that accompanies a representation of a great horned serpent (fig. 100) may be interpreted as the shrine house of that monster, and it is to be mentioned that this shrine appears to be surrounded by radial lines representing curved sticks

---

[1] Fewkes, Hopi Shrines Near the East Mesa, Arizona, pp. 346–375.

[2] The sand picture made by the Antelope priest is regarded as a house of the rain gods depicted upon it.

[3] *Seventeenth Ann. Rept. Bur. Amer. Ethn.*, pt. 2.

like those set around sand pictures of the Snake and Antelope altars of the Snake ceremonies at Walpi.[1]

It is suggested that the figure below the mountain sheep (see fig. 18) and the circles with dots accompanying the butterfly and bird designs may also represent shrines. Attention is also called to the fact that each of the six animal figures of the elaborate butterfly vase (pl. 90, c) is accompanied by a rectangular design representing a shrine in which feathers are visible.

FIG. 100.—Horned snake with conventionalized shrine.

The general forms of these shrines are shown in figures 101 and 102. The one shown in figure 103 is especially instructive from its association with a highly conventionalized animal.

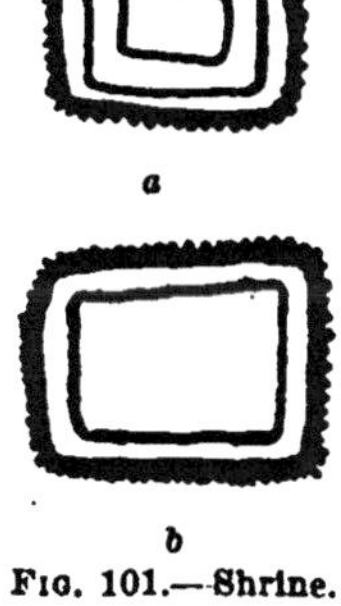

The Sikyatki epoch of Hopi ceramics is more closely allied to early Keresan[2] than to ancient Tanoan, and has many likenesses to modern Keresan pottery. In fact, none of the distinctive figures have yet been found on true Tanoan ware in any great numbers. There appear also no evidences of incre-

a

b

FIG. 101.—Shrine.

[1] The author has a drawing of the Snake altar at Michongnovi by an Indian, in which these crooks are not represented vertically but horizontally, a position illustrating a common method of drawing among primitive people who often represent vertical objects on a horizontal plane. An illustration of this is seen in pictures of a medicine bowl where the terraces on the rim normally vertical are drawn horizontally.

[2] In using this term the author refers to an extreme area in one corner of which still survive pueblos, the inhabitants of which speak Keres.

ments peculiar to the Little Colorado culture center of which Zuñi is the modern survival; consequently we look in vain for evidence of early communication between these two centers; possibly Sikyatki fell before Zuñi attained any prominence in the Little Colorado area.[1]

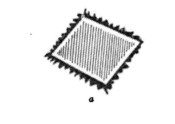

FIG. 102.—Shrine.

SYMBOLS INTRODUCED FROM SAN JUAN RIVER SETTLEMENTS

Although the majority of Hopi priests declare that the earliest clan to settle Walpi was the Bear, coming from the east, by far the largest number of early colonists are said to belong to the Snake people which came from Tokonabi and other great settlements on tributaries of the San Juan in northern Arizona. The route of their migration is fairly well known from legendary sources supported in late years by some limited excavations that have been made in ruins along its course, so that we know something of the character of the Snake pottery and the symbols, which these early colonists brought to the Bear settlement at the base of the East Mesa. These are not unlike those found along the San Juan and its tributaries from the Mesa Verde to Wukoki near the Black Falls on the Little Colorado, west of the Hopi Mesa.

This ware is commonly either black and white, or

FIG. 103. — Conventionalized winged bird with shrine.

red, and can be readily distinguished from that of Sikyatki by the wealth of geometrical decorations and the poverty of such animal figures as birds, reptiles, and insects. The designs of that early epoch appear to be uniform and hardly distinctive from those that occur in all parts of the Southwest.

[1] There is no published evidence in Zuñi legends that Sikyatki received increments from that pueblo.

We may judge of the character of the symbols and designs on pottery from the San Juan and from the ruins of Wukoki on the Black Falls of Little Colorado. It is characterized by an abundance of geometric figures and an almost total absence of life forms or painted figures of men and animals. The pottery is thin, well made, and sometimes colored red, but the majority of specimens are gray or black-and-white ware not especially different from a widespread type occurring pretty generally throughout the Southwest. Coiled and incised ware is more abundant than smooth painted, but these are not as varied in form as later examples. There is no evidence available that there was any very great difference between the Hopi pottery decorations of the first epoch and that of contemporary time in the Southwest. When the Snake clans arrived at Walpi they found the village of Bear people living on the terrace at the base of the East Mesa, possessed of a symbolism like that of Sikyatki. The combined clans, Bear and Snake, were later joined by the Horn and Flute, and it is not unlikely that some of the likenesses between the pottery symbols of the settlement on the terrace below Walpi and Sikyatki may have developed about this time.[1]

The designs on the ceramics of the Snake clans are best illustrated by the prehistoric pottery from ruins and cliff-dwellings in Utah and along the San Juan area, where geometrical patterns far outnumber those representing life forms. This does not deny that many of the pieces of pottery from this region are finely made, equal in technique perhaps to some of the Sikyatki, but the geometric designs on San Juan pottery and that from Sikyatki are radically different. This difference conforms with tradition that the Snake clans left their homes at Tokonabi, in the San Juan region, and came to Hopi after the foundation of Sikyatki, which had probably developed its beautiful ceramic art before Walpi was settled. There is no evidence that the potters of the Snake clan ever introduced any modification in the symbolic decoration of pottery by the women of Sikyatki.

Symbols Introduced by the Snake People

The designs on pottery taken from prehistoric ruins of pueblos or villages once inhabited by the Snake clans claim the archeologist's especial attention. These clans were the most important early additions to the Hopi villages and no doubt influenced early Hopi symbolism. There is little trace in early pottery that can be recognized as peculiar to the Snake. The Snake clans formerly lived at Betatakin, Kitsiel, and neighboring ruins.

---

[1] Since the author's work at Sikyatki, excavations have been made by the Field Columbian Museum at this ruin, but nothing bearing on the relations of symbols has been published so far as known to the writer.

Among many significant differences that occur between the designs on pottery from the ruins in Navaho National Monument and those of Sikyatki may be mentioned the rarity of bird designs and the conventional feathers above described. Parallel lines and triangles have been found on the pottery from Kitsiel and Betatakin. Terraced figures are common; spirals are rare. Pottery designs from this region are simpler and like those of the Mesa Verde cliffhouses and the ruins along the San Juan River. Not only do the designs on prehistoric Sikyatki pottery have little resemblance to those from Tokonabi, a former home of the Snake clan, but the pottery from this region of Arizona is of coarser texture and different color. It is the same as that of the San Juan area, the decorations on which are about uniform with those from the Mesa Verde and Chelly Canyon. The best vases and bowls are of red or black-and-white ware.

In the pottery symbols of the clans that lived at Tokonabi (Kitsiel, Betatakin, etc.) the archaic predominated. The passage architecturally from the fragile-walled dwelling into Prudden's pueblo "unit type" had taken place, but the pottery had not yet been greatly modified. Even after the Snake clans moved to Wukoki, near the Black Falls of the Little Colorado, we still find the survival of geometrical designs characteristic of the prepuebloan epoch. Consequently when the Snake clans came to Walpi and joined the Hopi they brought no new symbols and introduced no great changes in symbols. The influence of the clans from the north was slight—too small to greatly influence the development of Hopi symbolism.

TANOAN EPOCH

The Tanoan epoch in the chronology of Hopi pottery symbolism is markedly different from the Keresan. It began with the influx of Tanoan clans, either directly or by way of Zuñi and the Little Colorado, being represented in modern times by the early creations of Hano women, like Nampeo. It is clearly marked and readily distinguished from the Sikyatki epoch, being well represented in eastern museums by pottery collected from Hano, the Tewan pueblo on the East Mesa.

Migrations of Tanoan clans into the Hopi country began very early in Hopi history, but waves of colonists with Tanoan kinship came to Walpi at the close of the seventeenth century as a result of the great rebellion (1680), when the number of colonists from the Rio Grande pueblos was very large. The Badger, Kachina, Asa, and Hano clans seem to have been the most numerous and important in modifying sociological conditions, especially at the East Mesa of the Hopi. Some of these came directly to Walpi, others entered by way of Zuñi, and still others by way of Awatobi. They brought with them Tanoan and Keresan symbolism and Little Colorado elements, all of which were incorporated. The Tanoan symbols are very difficult to differentiate individually but created a considerable modification in the artistic products, as a whole.

The symbolism that the colonists from the Little Colorado settlements brought to Walpi was mixed in character, containing certain Gila Valley elements. Among the last-mentioned were increments derived directly from Zuñi, as shown in the symbolism of their pottery. Among the most important thus introduced were contributions of the Asa, Kachina, Badger, and Butterfly clans. The most important element from the Little Colorado clans that originally came from the Gila Valley (Palatkwabi) are those connected with the plumed serpent.[1] It is possible to trace successive epochs in the history of ceramic decoration in the Little Colorado ruins and to identify, in a measure, the clans with which these epochs were associated, but to follow out this identification in this paper would take me too far afield and lead into a discussion of areas far distant from the Hopi, for it belongs more especially to the history of ceramic decorations of Zuñi decoration and composition.[2] In the present article all the Little Colorado influences are treated as belonging to the Tanoan epoch, which seems to have been the dominant one in the Little Colorado when emigration, comparatively modern in time, began to Hopi.

Symbols Introduced from the Little Colorado

After the destruction of Sikyatki there was apparently a marked deterioration in the excellence of Hopi ceramics, which continued as late as the overthrow of Awatobi, when the Sikyatki epoch ceased. Shortly before that date and for a few years later there was a notable influx of foreigners into Hopiland; a number of southern clans from the Little Colorado successively joined the Hopi, bringing with them cultural conceptions and symbolic designs somewhat different from those existing previously to their advent. Among these clans are those known in migration legends as the Patki peoples. Although we can not distinguish a special Patki epoch in Hopi ceramics, we have some ideas of the nature of Patki symbolism from large collections from Homolobi, Chevlon, and Chavez Pass.

[1] The Tanoan people (clans) also introduced a horned snake, but different in symbolism from that of the Patki clans.

[2] The oldest pottery in the Zuñi Valley belongs to the same group as that of the oldest Little Colorado ruins and shows marked Gila Valley symbolism. The modern pottery of Zuñi is strongly influenced by Tanoan characters. As these have been transmitted to Hopi they are considered under the term "Tanoan epoch," derived from Little Colorado settlements to which Zuñi culturally belongs.

From traditions and ceremonial objects now in use we also know
something of the nature of the objective symbols they introduced into
Walpi, and we can detect some of these on pottery and other objects
used in ceremonies at Walpi. Some of these symbols did not come
directly from the Little Colorado ruins, but went first to Awatobi
and from there to Walpi [1] after the destruction of the former pueblo
in the autumn of the year 1700. The arrival of southern clans at the
East Mesa with their characteristic symbols occurred approximately
in the seventeenth century, about 200 years after the date of the
discovery of Hopi by Tovar. Awatobi received the Rabbit, Tobacco,
and other clans from this migration from the south between the years
1632 and 1700, and Walpi received the Patki shortly after or at the
same time the Hano clans came from the far east. The similarities
in ancient pottery from the Little Colorado and that belonging to the
Sikyatki epoch can not be ascribed to anything more profound than
superficial contact. It is not probable that the ancient pottery of
Awatobi or that of Kawaika and other Keres pueblos on the Awatobi
mesa or in the adjacent plain was modified in any considerable degree
by incoming clans from the south, but survived the Sikyatki epoch
a century after Sikyatki had been destroyed.

The advent of the clans from the Little Colorado into the Hopi
country was too late to seriously affect the classic period of Hopi
ceramics; it appears also not to have exerted any great influence on
later times. Extensive excavations made at Homolobi, Chevlon, and
Chavez Pass have revealed much pottery which gives a good idea of
the symbolism characteristic of the clans living along this valley,
which resembles in some respects the classic Hopi pottery of the time
of Sikyatki, but several of these likenesses date back to a time before
the union of the Hopi and Little Colorado clans. As a rule the bird
figures on pottery from Homolobi, Chevlon, Chavez Pass, and other
representative Little Colorado ruins are more realistic and less conventionalized and complex than those from Sikyatki. The peculiar
forms of feathers found so constantly in the latter do not occur in the
former, nor does the sky-band with its dependent bird figure ever
occur on Little Colorado ware. We are here dealing with less-devel-
oped conventionalism, a cruder art, and less specialized symbolism.
Even if the colors of the pottery did not at once separate them, the
expert can readily declare whether he is dealing with a bowl from
Sikyatki or Homolobi. There are, to be sure, likenesses, but well-
marked differences of local development. The resemblances and differences in the case of bird figures on prehistoric Hopi ware and that
from the ruins on the Little Colorado can be readily shown by considering figures 105, 106, and 107, found at Homolobi and Chevlon, and

---

[1] Pakatcomo in the plain below Walpi was their first Hopi settlement.

the corresponding preceding bird figures. It may be interesting to
instance another example. Figure 104 shows a lateral view of a bird
with wings extended, bearing marginal dentations representing feathers on the breast and a tail composed of four triangular feathers and
two eyes, each with iris and pupil. The upper and lower jaws in this
figure are extended to form a beak, as is customary in bird designs
from the Little Colorado ruins, but never found at Sikyatki. In
figure 105 we have another lateral view of a characteristic bird design

Fig. 104.—Lateral view of bird with double eyes.

from the Little Colorado region, and figures 106 and 107 show hourglass bodies, a special feature of the same region.

In the same way many other distinctive characteristics separating
figures of animals from the two regions might be mentioned. Those
above given may suffice to show that each is distinctive and in a way
specialized in its development, but the main reason to believe that
the clans from the Little Colorado never affected the symbolism of
Sikyatki is the fact that the latter ruin was destroyed before these
clans joined the Hopi villages.

The ruins Homolobi and Chevlon were probably inhabited well into historic times, although there is no archeological evidence that artifacts from them were modified by European influences. The symbolism on pottery shows that their culture was composite and seems to have been the result of acculturation from both south and east. Some of the clans, as the Tobacco, that peopled these settlements joined Awatobi before its overthrow, while others settled at Pakatcomo, the ruins of which near Walpi are still visible, and later united with the people of the largest village of the East Mesa. So far as known, Sikyatki had been destroyed before any considerable number of people had entered the Hopi country from the Little Colorado,[1] the event occurring comparatively late in history.

FIG. 105.—Lateral view of bird with double eyes.

The pottery from the Little Colorado differs from prehistoric Hopi ware much less with respect to geometrical designs than life forms. The break in the encircling line, or, as it is called, the life gate, which is almost universally found on the ancient Hopi vases, bowls, dippers, and other objects, occurs likewise on pottery from Little Colorado ruins. Some of the encircling lines from this region have more than one break, and in one instance the edges of the break have appendages, a rare feature found in both prehistoric Hopi and Little Colorado ware.[2]

The influence of Keres culture on Zuñi may be shown in several ways, thus: A specimen of red ware from a shrine on Thunder Mountain, an old Zuñi site, is decorated with symbolic feathers recalling those on Sikyatki ware ascribed to eastern influence. The nonappearance of Keres and Tewa symbols on ancient pottery from the Zuñi Valley ruins, Heshotauthla and Hálonawan, and their

---

[1] As has been pointed out, the designs on ancient Zuñi ware are closely related to those of ruins farther down the Little Colorado, and are not Hopi. Modern Zuñi as well as modern Hopi pueblos were influenced by Keres and Tewa culture superimposed on the preexisting culture, which largely came from the Gila.

[2] No invariable connection was found in the relative position of this break and figures of birds or other animals inclosed by the broken band. The gaps in different encircling bands on the same bowl are either diametrically opposite each other or separated by a quadrant, a variation that would appear to indicate that they were not made use of in a determination of the orientation of the vessel while in ceremonial use, as is true of certain baskets of modern Navaho.

existence in the mountain shrine above mentioned, implies that the latter settlement is more modern, and that the eastern clans united with preexisting Little Colorado clans comparatively late in its history. The first settlements in Zuñi Valley were made by colonists from the Gila. There are several ceremonies in the Walpi ritual which, like the New Fire, although immediately derived from Awatobi, came originally from Little Colorado pueblos, and other cere-

Fɪɢ. 106.—Bird with double eyes.

monies came directly to Walpi from the same original source. Among the former are those introduced by the Piba (Tobacco) clan, which brought to Walpi a secret fraternity called the Tataukyamu. This brotherhood came directly from Awatobi, but the Tobacco clan from which it was derived once lived in a pueblo on the Little Colorado, now a ruin at Chevlon, midway between Holbrook and Winslow.[1] The identification of the Chevlon ruin with the historic

[1] The author has the following evidence that the inhabitants of the village at Chevlon were the historic Chipias. The Hopi have a legend that the large ruin called Tcipiaiya by the Zuñi was also situated on a river midway between Walpi and Zuñi. The Hopi also say that the Chevlon pueblo was inhabited by the Piba (Tobacco) clan and that the Awatobi chief, Tapolo, who brought the Tataukyamu fraternity to Walpi from Awatobi, belonged to the Tobacco clan. The Tewa name of the Tataukyamu is Tcipiaiyu, or "men from Tcipia."

Chipias has an important bearing on the age of the Little Colorado ruins, for Padre Arvide, a Franciscan missionary, was killed in 1632 by the Chipias, who lived west of Zuñi. In other words, their pueblo was then inhabited.

We know that the Piba joined Awatobi before 1700, or the year it was destroyed; consequently the desertion of the Chevlon ruin (Chipiaya, or Tcipiaiya) evidently occurred between 1632 and 1700,

FIG. 107.—Two birds with rain clouds.

not so much on account of Apache inroads as from fear of punishment by the Spaniards.[1] As no clans from the other large pueblo on the Little Colorado or Homolobi joined Awatobi, we can not definitely fix the date that this group fled to the north, but it was probably not long after the time the Chevlon clans migrated to Awatobi, from which it follows that the Little Colorado settlements were inhabited up to the middle of the seventeenth century. While the

[1] It is known from an inscription on El Morro that a punitive expedition to avenge the death of Father Letrado was sent out under Lujan in the spring of 1632, hence the guilty inhabitants may have abandoned their settlement and departed for Hopi at about that time.

Little Colorado clans did not influence the Sikyatki pottery, they did affect the potters of Awatobi to a limited extent and introduced some symbols into Walpi in the middle of the seventeenth and eighteenth centuries. Among these influences may be mentioned those derived from Awatobi after its destruction in 1700. It is not possible to state definitely what modifications in pottery symbols were introduced into Walpi by the potters of the clans from Awatobi and the Little Colorado. Possibly no considerable modification resulted from their advent, as there was already more or less similarity in the pottery from these geographical localities. The southern clans introduced some novelties in ceremonies, especially in the Winter Solstice and New-fire festivals and in the rites of the Horned Serpent at the Spring Equinox.

Symbols Introduced by the Badger and Kachina Clans

As the clans which came to the Hopi country from Zuñi were comparatively late arrivals of Tewa colonists long after the destruction of Sikyatki, their potters exerted no influence on the Sikyatki potters. The ancient Hopi ceramic art had become extinct when the clans from Awatobi, the pueblos on the Little Colorado, and the late Tewa, united with the Walpi settlement on the East Mesa. The place whence we can now obtain information of the character of the symbolism of the Asa, Butterfly, Badger, and other Tewan clans is in certain ceremonies at Sichomovi, a pueblo near Walpi, settled by clans from Zuñi and often called the Zuñi pueblo by the Hopi. One of the Sichomovi ceremonies celebrated at Oraibi and Sichomovi on the East Mesa, in which we may find survivals of the earliest Tewa and Zuñi symbolism, is called the Owakülti. The Sichomovi variant of the Owakülti shows internal sociologic relation to the Butterfly or Buli (Poli) clan resident in Awatobi before its fall. This statement is attested by certain stone slabs excavated from Awatobi mounds, on which are painted butterfly symbols. The Walpi Lalakoñti, first described by the author and Mr. Owens in 1892, has also survivals of Awatobi designs. It appears that while it is not easy to trace any of the rich symbolism of Awatobi directly into Walpi pottery, it is possible to discover close relations between certain Awatobi symbols and others still employed in Walpi ceremonials. Sikyatki and Awatobi were probably inhabited synchronously and as kindred people had a closely allied or identical symbolism; there is such a close relation between the designs on pottery from the two ruins that Awatobi symbols introduced into Walpi have a close likeness to those of Sikyatki.[1]

---

[1] The Buli (Poli) clan is probably Tewa, as the word indicates, which would show that Tewa as well as Keres clans lived at Awatobi. No legend mentions Buli clans at Sikyatki, but several traditions locate them at Awatobi.

The natural conservatism in religious rites of all kinds has brought it about that many of the above-mentioned designs, although abandoned in secular life of the Hopi, still persist in paraphernalia used in ceremonies. It is therefore pertinent to discuss some of these religious symbols with an idea of discovering whether they are associated with certain clans or ruins, and if so what light they shed on prehistoric migrations. In other words, here the ethnologists can afford us much information bearing on the significance of prehistoric symbols.

One great difficulty in interpreting the prehistoric pictures of supernaturals depicted on ancient pottery by a comparison of the religious paraphernalia of the modern Hopi is a complex nomenclature of supernatural beings that has been brought about by the perpetuation or survival of different clan names for the same being even after union of those clans. Thus we find the same Sky god with many others all practically aliases of one common conception. To complicate the matter still more, different attributal names are also sometimes used. The names Alosaka, Muyinwu, and Talatumsi are practically different designations of the same supernatural, while Tunwup, Ho, and Shalako appear to designate the same Sky-god personage. Cultus heroines, as the Marau mana, Shalako mana, Palahiko mana, and others, according as we follow one or another of the dialects, Keres or Tewa, are used interchangeably. This diversity in nomenclature has introduced a complexity in the Hopi mythology which is apparent rather than real in the Hopi Pantheon, as their many names would imply.[1] The great nature gods of sky and earth, male and female, lightning and germination, no doubt arose as simple transfer of a germinative idea applied to cosmic phenomena and organic nature. The earliest creation myths were drawn largely from analogies of human and animal birth. The innumerable lesser or clan gods are naturally regarded as offspring of sky and earth, and man himself is born from Mother Earth. He was not specially created by a Great Spirit, which was foreign to Indians unmodified by white influences.

As the number of bird designs on Sikyatki pottery far outnumber representations of other animals it is natural to interpret them by modern bird symbols or by modern personations of birds, many examples of which are known to the ethnological student of the Hopi.

In one of a series of dances at Powamû, which occurs in February, men and boys personate the eagle, red hawk, humming bird, owl, cock, hen, mocking bird, quail, hawk, and other birds, each appropriately dressed, imitating cries, and wearing an appropriate mask

---

[1] A unification of names of these gods would have resulted when the languages of the many different clans had been fused in religions, as the language was in secular usage. The survival of component names of Hopi gods is paralleled in the many ancient religions.

of the birds they represent. In a dance called Pamurti, a ceremony celebrated annually at Sichomovi, and said to have been derived from Zuñi, personations of the same birds appear, the men of Walpi contributing to the performance. Homovi, one of the Hopi Indians who took part, made colored pictures representing all these birds, which may be found reproduced in the author's article on Hopi katcinas.[1]

In the Hopi cosmogony the Sky god is thought to be father of all gods and human beings, and when personations of the subordinate supernaturals occur they are led to the pueblo by a personator of this great father of all life. The celebrations of the Powamû, at the East Mesa of the Hopi, represent the return of the ancestors or kachinas of Walpi, while the Pamurti is the dramatization of the return of the kachinas of Sichomovi whose ancestors were Zuñi kin.

Life figures or animal forms, as birds, serpents, and insects, depicted on Little Colorado pottery differ considerably from those on Sikyatki ware. Take, for instance, bird designs, the most abundant life forms on ancient pueblo pottery on the Little Colorado, as well as at Sikyatki. It needs but a glance at the figures of the former to show how marked the differences are. The leader of the kachinas in the Powamû, which celebrates the return of these ancestral gods to the pueblo, Walpi, wears an elaborate dress and helmet with appended feathers. He is led into the village by a masked man personating Eototo.[2]

SYMBOLS INTRODUCED FROM AWATOBI

The women saved at Awatobi in the massacre of 1700, according to a legend, brought to Walpi the paraphernalia of a ceremony still observed, called the Mamzrauti. Naturally we should expect to find old Awatobi symbolism on this paraphernalia, which is still in use. The cultus heroine of the Mamzrauti is the Corn-mist maid, known by the name of Shalako mana or Palahiko mana.[3] We have several representations of this maid and their resemblance to the pictures of Shalako mana depicted by Hano potters would imply a common Tanoan origin.

SHALAKO MANA

The most common figure on the third epoch of Hopi pottery, commonly called modern Tewa and manufactured up to 1895 by Nampeo, a Hano potter, is a representation of the Corn maid, Shalako mana,

[1] *Twenty-first Ann. Rept. Bur. Amer. Ethn.*

[2] Ibid., p. 76. Eototo, also called Masauû, was the tutelary of Sikyatki, as Alosaka or Muyinwu was of Awatobi.

[3] A somewhat similar personage to Shalako mana in Aztec ceremonies was called Xalaquia (Shalakia).

who, as shown, is the same personage as Marau mana and Palahiko mana in the festival of the Mamzrauti derived from Awatobi. The symbol of this goddess is instructive and easily recognized in its many variations. Her picture on Hano pottery is shown in figure 108.

The most striking features of her symbolism, brought out in plate 89, are terraced bodies representing rain clouds on the head, an ear of maize symbol on the forehead, curved lines over the mouth, chevrons on the cheeks, conventionalized wings, and feathered garment. It is also not uncommon to find carved representations of

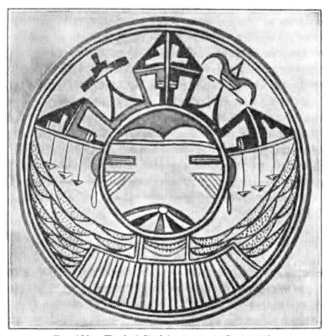

FIG. 108.—Head of Shalako mana, or Corn maid.

squash blossoms occupying the same positions as the whorls of hair on the heads of Hopi maidens.

The Shalakotaka male is likewise a common design readily recognized on modern pottery. Particularly abundant are figures of the mask of a Kohonino god, allied to Shalako, which is likewise called a kachina, best shown in paraphernalia of the Mamzrauti ceremony.

It sometimes happens in Hopi dramatization that pictures of supernatural beings and idols of the same take the place of personations by priests. For instance, instead of a girl or a woman representing the Corn maid, this supernatural is depicted on a slab of wood or represented by a wooden idol. One of the best-known figures of the Corn maid (Shalako mana) is here introduced (pl. 89) to

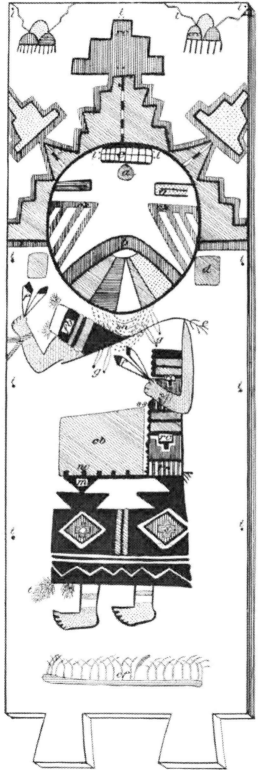

SHALAKO MANA, CORN MAID (FROM TABLET

illustrate the relation of old Awatobi and existing Hopi symbolism; a modern figure (108) of this Corn maid, painted on a wooden slab, is sometimes carried by the Walpi women in their dance. Figures of the Awatobi germ god, Alosaka, otherwise called Muyinwû,[1] are depicted on the slabs used by most of the women at that time.

The different designs on the slab under consideration (pl. 89) are indicated by letters and explained as follows: *a* represents a circular fragment of the haliotis or abalone shell hanging midway from a figure of an ear of corn, *c*. The cheeks are tattooed or painted with characteristic figures, *cb*, the eyes rectangular of different colors. The letter *d* is a representation of a wooden ear pendant, a square, flat body covered on one side with a mosaic of turquoise sometimes arranged in figures. The letter *e* is the end of a string by which the ceremonial blanket is tied over the left shoulder, the right arm being free, as shown in the illustration. Over the right shoulder, however, is thrown a ceremonial embroidered kilt, *fb*.

The objects in the hands represent feathers and recall one type of the conventional feathers figured in the preceding pages. The letters *fr* represent falling rain embroidered on the rim of the ceremonial blanket and *rc* the terraced rain clouds which in *arc* become rounded above; *g* represents a turquoise at the end of a string of turquoise suspended from shell necklaces *sn*; *m* represents the butterfly and is practically identical with the decorations on dados of old Hopi houses; *s* represents a star; *sb* represents shell bracelets, many examples of which occur in ruins along the Little Colorado; *ss* is supposed to have replaced the key patterns which some authorities identify as sprouting beans. There are commonly nine rectangular markings, *nc*, on the upper border of the embroidered region of ceremonial blankets and kilts, each of which represents either a month or a day, by some said to refer to ceremonial or germ periods.[2]

The Shalako mana figures have not yet been found in the unmodified Little Colorado ware, but homologous figures have been found in the Rio Grande area.

The design (pl. 88, *d*) with a horn on the left side of the head and a rectangle on the right, the face being occupied by a terrace figure from which hang parallel lines, reminds one of the " coronets " worn on the head by the *Lakone* maids (manas) in the Walpi Basket dance of the Lalakonti. The horn in the coronet is without terminal appendages, although a feather is tied to it, and the rectangle of plate 88, *d*, is replaced by radiating slats spotted and pointed at

[1] An account of this dance with details of the nine days' ceremony as presented in the major or October variant will be found in the *American Anthropologist*, July, 1892. The minor or Winter ceremony, in which the Corn maids are personated by girls, is published in the same journal for 1900. The Corn maid has several aliases in this ceremony, among which are Shalako mana, Palahiko mana, and Marau mana.

[2] This Corn maid is one of the most common figures represented by dolls.

their ends, said to represent the sunflower. The whole design in plate 88, *d*, represents a bird,[1] recalling that of the figure Marautiyo on one of the appended slabs of the altar of the Walpi Marau ceremony. In this altar figure we find not only a horn on the left side of the head, but also a rectangular design on the right.

On the corresponding right-hand side of this altar we have a picture of Marau mana (Shalako mana). It will thus appear that when compared with the Lakone coronet the figure on the Shongopovi bowl represents a female being, whereas when compared with the figure on the Marau altar it resembles a male being. There is, therefore, something wrong in my comparison. But the fact remains that there survive in the two woman's festivals—Lakone maid's coronet and Marau altar—resemblances to prehistoric Hopi designs from Shongopovi. Moreover, it is known that the Marau fetishes are stated by the chief Saliko to have been introduced from Awatobi into Walpi by her ancestor who was saved at the massacre of that town in 1700.

The life figures of the Tanoan epoch, or that following the overthrow of Sikyatki, can be made out by a study of modern Hano pottery. Perhaps the most complex of these is that of the Corn maid, Shalako mana. Shalako mana plays a great rôle in the Mamzrauti, a ceremony derived from Awatobi, and figures representing her are common designs made on Hano pottery. Designs representing this being are common on the peculiar basket plaques made at the Middle Mesa and dolls of her are abundant. The constant presence of her pictures on basket plaques at the Middle Mesa would also seem to show an ancient presence in the Hopi country, and indicate an identity of pottery designs from ancient Shumopavi with those from the East Mesa and Awatobi.[2]

One of her modern Walpi ceremonies has such pronounced Awatobi symbolism that it may be instanced as showing derivation; viz, the New-fire festival.[3] The women of the Marau and the men of the Tataukyamû regard themselves kindred, and taunt each other, as only friends may without offence, in this festival, and the Tataukyamû often introduce a burlesque Shalako mana into their performances.

---

[1] The two parallel lines on the two outside tail feathers recall the markings on the face of the War god Puükoñghoya.

[2] A personation of Shalako mana at Oraibi, according to Mr. H. R. Voth, came from Mishongnovi. This conforms exactly with the legends that state the Mamsrauti may have been introduced into Mishongnovi from Awatobi, for at the division of the captive women at Maski many of the women went to that pueblo.

[3] See Fewkes, The New-fire Ceremony at Walpi, pp. 80–138. The New-fire rites at Walpi are celebrated in November, when four societies, Aaltû, Wüwütcimtû, Tataukyamû, and Kwakwantû, take part. As in all new-fire ceremonies, phallic or generative rites are prominent, the Wüwütcimtû and Tataukyamû who kindle the fire being conspicuous in these rites. Their bodies have phallic emblems painted on them and the latter bear Zuñi symbols.

The designs painted on the bodies and heads of several modern dolls representing Corn maids are symbols whose history is very ancient in the tribe. For instance, those of feathers date back to prehistoric times, and terraced designs representing rain clouds are equally ancient. The dolls of the Corn maid (Shalako mana) present a variety of forms of feathers and the headdresses of many dolls represent kachinas, and show feathers sometimes represented by sticks on which characteristic markings are painted, but more often they represent symbols.[1]

SYMBOLS OF HANO CLANS

Hano, as is well known, is a Tewan pueblo, situated on the East Mesa, which was the last great body of Tewa colonists to migrate to Hopiland. While other Tewa colonists lost their language and became Hopi, the inhabitants of Hano still speak Tewa and still preserve some of their old ceremonies, and consequently many of their own symbols. Here were found purest examples of the Tanoan epoch.

The potters of clans introduced symbols on their ware radically different from those of Sikyatki, the type of the epoch of the finest Hopi ceramics, and replaced it by Tewan designs which characterize Hopi pottery from 1710 to 1895, when a return was suddenly made to the ancient type through the influence of Nampeo. At that date she began to cleverly imitate Sikyatki ware and abandoned *de toto* symbols introduced by Hano and other Tewa clans.

Fortunately there exist good collections of the Tewa epoch of Hopi ceramics, but the ever-increasing demand by tourists for ancient ware induced Nampeo to abandon the Tewa clan symbols she formerly employed and to substitute those of ancient Sikyatki.[2]

The majority of the specimens of Hano pottery, like those of the Tanoan epoch to which it belongs, are decorated with pictures of clan ancients called kachinas. These have very little resemblance to designs characteristic of the Sikyatki epoch. They practically belong to the same type as those introduced by Kachina, Asa, and Badger peoples. One of the most common of these is the design above dis-

---

[1] The designs on the wooden slats carried by women in the dance known as the Marau ceremony are remarkably like some of those on Awatobi and Sikyatki pottery.

[2] Much of the pottery offered for sale by Harvey and other dealers in Indian objects along the Santa Fe Railroad in Arizona and New Mexico is imitation prehistoric Hopi ware made by Nampeo. The origin of this transformation was due partly to the author, who in the year named was excavating the Sikyatki ruins and graves. Nampeo and her husband, Lesou, came to his camp, borrowed paper and pencil, and copied many of the ancient symbols found on the pottery vessels unearthed, and these she has reproduced on pottery of her own manufacture many times since that date. It is therefore necessary, at the very threshold of our study, to urge discrimination between modern and ancient pottery in the study of Hopi ware, and careful elimination of imitations. The modern pottery referred to is easily distinguished from the prehistoric, inasmuch as the modern is not made with as much care or attention to detail as the ancient. Also the surface of the modern pottery is coated with a thin slip which crackles in firing.

cussed representing Shalako mana, the Corn maid, shown in figure 109. In this figure we have the face represented by a circle in the center and many lenticular figures arranged in rows attached to the

FIG. 109.—Head of Kokle, or Earth woman.

neck and shoulders corresponding to the appendages explained in figure 108. It is said in the legends that when the Corn maid appeared to men she was enveloped in fleecy clouds and wore a feathered garment. These are indicated by the curved figures covered with dots and the parallel lines on the body. Feather symbols recalling those of the Sikyatki epoch hang from appendages to the head representing rain clouds.

FIG. 110.—Head of Hahaiwugti, or Earth woman.

In figure 109 we have a representation of the head with surrounding clouds, and portions of the body of a kachina, called Kokle, who is personated in Winter ceremonies. It is instructive to note that this figure has symbols on the head that recall the Sikyatki epoch. The ancient Tewan earth goddess, Hahaiwugti, is represented in figure 110. She appears also in figure 111, where her picture is painted on a ladle, the handle of which represents an ancient Tewan clown called by the Hano people Paiakyamû.

The War god, Püükon hoya, also a Tewan incorporation in the Hopi pantheon, appears frequently on pottery of the Tanoan epoch, as shown in figure 112. This figure, painted on a terra-cotta slab, is identified by the two parallel marks on each cheek.

CONCLUSION

In the preceding pages an attempt has been made to trace the chronological sequence of pottery symbols in Hopiland by pointing out distinct epochs in cultural history and correlating the sociology of the tribe. This takes for granted that the pottery symbols characteristic of this people are directly connected with certain clans. There have from time to time been sudden changes in symbols, or previous designs have suddenly disappeared and others have taken their places, as well as a slow development of existing symbols into more complicated forms. There persist everywhere survivals of old prepuebloan symbols inherited from the past and a creation of new products of Hopi environment not found elsewhere.

FIG. 111.—Ladle with clown carved on handle and Earth woman on bowl.

FIG. 112.—Püükon hoya, little War god.

The author will close this paper with a brief theoretical account of the unwritten culture history of Hopi, part of which explains certain pottery symbols. If we take that segment of southwestern history extending from the earliest to the present, we find evidences of the existence of a prepuebloan culture existing before terraced houses were built or circular kivas had been used for ceremonial purposes. This epoch was antecedent to the construction of the great walled compounds of the Gila, illustrated by Casa Grande. At that epoch known as the prepuebloan there extended from Utah to the Mexican boundary and from the Colorado to the Rio Grande a culture architecturally characterized by small fragile-walled houses not united or terraced. These houses were sometimes like pit dwellings, either partially or wholly subterranean. When above ground their walls were supported by upright logs in which canes or brushes were woven and covered with mud, the roofs being made of cedar bark or straw overlaid with adobe.

The pottery of this early prehistoric epoch was smooth, painted mainly with geometric patterns, corrugated, or indented. Rectilinear or curved lines constituted the majority of the superficial decorations and life designs were few or altogether wanting. In addition to these architectural and ceramic characteristics, this prepuebloan cultural stage was distinguished by many other features, to mention which would take us too far afield and would be out of place in this article. Evidences of this stage or epoch occur everywhere in the Southwest and survival of the archaic characters enumerated are evident in all subsequent epochs.

The so-called " unit type " or pure pueblo culture grew out of this early condition and was at first localized in northern New Mexico and southern Colorado, where it was autochthonous. Its essential feature is the terraced communal house and the simplest form of the pueblo, the " unit type," first pointed out by Dr. T. Mitchell Prudden—a combination of dwelling houses, with a man's house or kiva and a cemetery. The dwellings are made of stone or clay and are terraced, the kiva is subterranean and circular, embedded in or surrounded by other rooms. The " unit type " originated in Colorado and, spreading in all directions, replaced the preexisting houses with fragile walls. Colonists from its center extended down the San Juan to the Hopi country and made their way easterly across the Rio Grande and southerly to the headwaters of the Gila and Little Colorado, where they met other clans of specialized prepuebloan culture who had locally developed an architecture of Great House style characteristic of the Gila and Salt River Valleys.

The essential differences between the terraced pueblo and the previously existing fragile-walled house culture are two: The terraced architecture results from one house being constructed above another, the kiva or subterranean ceremonial room being separated or slightly removed from the secular houses.

An explanation of the origin of the terraced pueblo is evident. This form of house implies a limited site or a congestion of houses on a limited area. An open plain presents no limitation in lateral construction; there is plenty of room to expand in all directions to accommodate the enlargement which results as a settlement increases in population. In a cave conditions are otherwise; expansion is limited. When the floor of the cavern is once covered with rooms the only additions which can possibly be made must be vertically. In protection lies the cause of the development of a terraced architecture such as the pueblos show, for the early people con-

structed their fragile-walled habitations in a cavern, and as an enlargement of their numbers occurred they were obliged to construct
the terraced pueblos called cliff-dwellings, with rooms closely ap-
proximated and constructed in terraces. In the course of time these
cliff-dwellers moved out of their caverns into the river valleys or to
the mesa summits, carrying with them the terraced architecture,
which, born in caverns, survived in their new environment. This
explanation is of course hypothetical, but not wholly without a basis
in fact, for we find survivals of the prepuebloan architecture scat-
tered throughout the Southwest, especially on the periphery of the
terraced house area, as well as in the area itself. The ancient terraced house architecture is confined to a limited area, but around its
ancient border are people whose dwellings are characterized by
fragile-walled architecture. These are the survivals of the prepuebloan culture.

The environmental conditions along the San Juan and its tributaries in Colorado and New Mexico render it a particularly favorable
culture center from which the pure pueblo type may have originated,
and although observations have not yet gone far enough to prove
that here was the place of origin of the unit type, and therefore of
pueblo culture, there are strong indications that a fable of the
Pueblos, that they came from the caves in the north, is not without
legendary foundation so far as their origin is concerned.

The term "cliff-dwelling," once supposed to indicate a distinct
stage of development, refers only to the site and is a feature inadequate for classification or chronology. All cliff-dwellings do not
belong to the same structural type. There is little similarity save in
site between Spruce-tree House on the Mesa Verde, and Montezuma
Castle in the Verde Valley; the former belongs to the " pure pueblo
type," the latter to another class of buildings related to " compounds "
of the tributaries of the Gila and Salt River valleys.

AUTHORITIES CITED

Fewkes, Jesse Walter. Snake ceremonials at Walpi. *Journal of American Ethnology and Archæology*, vol. IV, pp. 1–126. Boston and New York, 1894.

——. Archeological expedition to Arizona in 1895. *Seventeenth Annual Report of the Bureau of American Ethnology*, pt. 2, pp. 519–742. Washington, 1898.

——. Winter solstice altars at Hano pueblo. *American Anthropologist*, n. s. vol. I, no. 2, pp. 251–276. New York, 1899.

——. The New-fire ceremony at Walpi. *American Anthropologist*, n. s. vol. II, no. 1, pp. 80–138. New York, 1900.

——. The lesser New-fire ceremony at Walpi. *American Anthropologist*, n. s. vol. III, no. 8, pp. 438–453. New York, 1901.

——. Hopi katcinas. *Twenty-first Annual Report of the Bureau of American Ethnology*, pp. 13–126. Washington, 1903.

——. Two summers' work in Pueblo ruins. *Twenty-second Annual Report of the Bureau of American Ethnology*, pt. 1, pp. 17–195. Washington, 1904.

——. Hopi ceremonial frames from Cañon de Chelly, Arizona. *American Anthropologist*, n. s. vol. VIII, no. 4, pp. 664–670. Lancaster, 1906.

——. Hopi shrines near the East Mesa, Arizona. *American Anthropologist*, n. s. vol. VIII, no. 2, pp. 346–375. Lancaster, 1908.

——. The butterfly in Hopi myth and ritual. *American Anthropologist*, n. s. vol. XII, no. 4, pp. 576–594. Lancaster, 1910.

Mallery, Garrick. On the pictographs of the North American Indians. *Fourth Annual Report of the Bureau of Ethnology*, pp. 13–256. Washington, 1886.

SAFARILAND
MODEL 27
SKU = 1097615
PART : 27-83-61
$ 52 ⁹⁹

MODEL 71 MAGAZINE POUCH
$ 15. - 2%,
800. 347. 1200

CPSIA information can be obtained at www.ICGtesting.com
Printed in the USA
BVOW061127210413

318641BV00004B/57/P

9 781104 730697